The Poetry of Sir John Denham

Sir John Denham FRS was born in 1614 or 1615 (an exact date cannot be corroborated) in Dublin, Ireland, the son of his like named father, Sir John Denham, Chief Baron of the Irish Exchequer, and his second wife Eleanor Moore, daughter of Garret Moore, 1st Viscount Moore.

Denham and was educated at Trinity College, Oxford and at Lincoln's Inn in London.

His literary career started with a tragedy, The Sophy, in 1641, followed a year later by his poem Cooper's Hill, probably his most famous work and a very early example of poetry devoted to the local description of the Thames Valley scenery surrounding his home at Egham in Surrey. During his career Denham was to return again and again to the work and write several versions to reflect the cultural and political upheavals of the Civil War.

A Royalist by nature this caused to hold him back during the Civil War but in 1642 he was appointed High Sheriff of Surrey and governor of Farnham Castle.

Whatever his politics it is as a poet that Denham, along with his fellow poet and contemporary Edmund Waller, exerted an influence on versification and poetical utterance and the great John Dryden thought their work to be the beginning of Augustan poetry.

In 1661 Denham was elected to Parliament for the seat of Old Sarum and became a Fellow of the Royal Society on May 20th, 1663, as well as a Knight of the Bath.

With the Restoration of Charles II Denham became Surveyor of the King's Works. He seemed to have no experience for this particular role and it is more likely it was awarded for past political services. John Webb, who, as Inigo Jones's deputy complained that "though Mr. Denham may, as most gentry, have some knowledge of the theory of architecture, he can have none of the practice and must employ another."

Although he could administrate nothing suggests any actual design work though his influence would undoubtedly have been taken into account.

Denham had an unhappy marriage, and his last years were clouded by advancing dementia. With Denham's increasing mental incapacity, Charles II requested in March 1669 that Christopher Wren be appointed Denham's "sole deputy"; Wren succeeded him as King's Surveyor upon his death two weeks later.

Sir John Denham died on March 19th, 1669 and is buried in Poets' Corner at Westminster Abbey.

Index of Contents

COOPER'S HILL

Sure there are poets which did never dream
Upon Parnassus, nor did taste the stream
Of Helicon; we therefore may suppose
Those made not poets, but the poets those,
And as courts make not kings, but kings the court,
So where the Muses and their train resort,
Parnassus stands; if I can be to thee
A poet, thou Parnassus art to me.
Nor wonder, if (advantaged in my flight,
By taking wing from thy auspicious height)
Through untraced ways and airy paths I fly,
More boundless in my fancy than my eye:
My eye which, swift as thought, contracts the space
That lies between, and first salutes the place
Crown'd with that sacred pile, so vast, so high,
That, whether 'tis a part of earth or sky,
Uncertain seems, and may be thought a proud
Aspiring mountain, or descending cloud.
Paul's, the late theme of such a Muse,[1] whose flight
Has bravely reach'd and soar'd above thy height:
Now shalt thou stand, though sword, or time, or fire,

Or zeal more fierce than they, thy fall conspire,
Secure, whilst thee the best of poets sings,
Preserved from ruin by the best of kings.
Under his proud survey the city lies,
And like a mist beneath a hill doth rise;
Whose state and wealth, the business and the crowd,
Seems at this distance but a darker cloud:
And is, to him who rightly things esteems,
No other in effect than what it seems:
Where, with like haste, though sev'ral ways, they run,
Some to undo, and some to be undone;
While luxury and wealth, like war and peace,
Are each the other's ruin and increase;
As rivers lost in seas some secret vein
Thence reconveys, there to be lost again.
O happiness of sweet retired content!
To be at once secure and innocent.
Windsor the next (where Mars with Venus dwells,
Beauty with strength) above the valley swells
Into my eye, and doth itself present
With such an easy and unforced ascent,
That no stupendous precipice denies
Access, no horror turns away our eyes:
But such a rise as doth at once invite
A pleasure and a rev'rence from the sight:
Thy mighty master's emblem, in whose face
Sate meekness, heighten'd with majestic grace;
Such seems thy gentle height, made only proud
To be the basis of that pompous load,
Than which, a nobler weight no mountain bears,
But Atlas only, which supports the spheres.
When Nature's hand this ground did thus advance,
'Twas guided by a wiser power than Chance;
Mark'd out for such an use, as if 'twere meant
T' invite the builder, and his choice prevent.
Nor can we call it choice, when what we choose,
Folly or blindness only could refuse.
A crown of such majestic towers doth grace
The gods' great mother, when her heavenly race
Do homage to her, yet she cannot boast,
Among that num'rous and celestial host.
More heroes than can Windsor; nor doth Fame's
Immortal book record more noble names.
Not to look back so far, to whom this isle
Owes the first glory of so brave a pile,
Whether to Cæsar, Albanact, or Brute,
The British Arthur, or the Danish Knute,
(Though this of old no less contest did move

Than when for Homer's birth seven cities strove)
(Like him in birth, thou shouldst be like in fame,
As thine his fate, if mine had been his flame),
But whosoe'er it was, Nature design'd
First a brave place, and then as brave a mind;
Not to recount those sev'ral kings, to whom
It gave a cradle, or to whom a tomb;
But thee, great Edward, and thy greater son[2]
(The lilies which his father wore, he won),
And thy Bellona,[3] who the consort came
Not only to thy bed, but to thy fame, so
She to thy triumph led one captive king,[4]
And brought that son, which did the second bring.
Then didst thou found that Order (whether love
Or victory thy royal thoughts did move),
Each was a noble cause, and nothing less
Than the design, has been the great success:
Which foreign kings, and emperors esteem
The second honour to their diadem.
Had thy great destiny but given thee skill
To know, as well as power to act her will,
That from those kings, who then thy captives were,
In after times should spring a royal pair
Who should possess all that thy mighty power,
Or thy desires more mighty, did devour:
To whom their better fate reserves whate'er
The victor hopes for, or the vanquish'd fear;
That blood, which thou and thy great grandsire shed,
And all that since these sister nations bled,
Had been unspilt, had happy Edward known.
That all the blood he spilt had been his own.
When he that patron chose, in whom are join'd
Soldier and martyr, and his arms confin'd
Within the azure circle, he did seem
But to foretell, and prophesy of him,
Who to his realms that azure round hath join'd,
Which Nature for their bound at first design'd;
That bound, which to the world's extremest ends,
Endless itself, its liquid arms extends.
Nor doth he need those emblems which we paint,
But is himself the soldier and the saint.
Here should my wonder dwell, and here my praise;
But my fix'd thoughts my wand'ring eye betrays,
Viewing a neighb'ring hill, whose top of late
A chapel crown'd, 'till in the common fate
Th' adjoining abbey fell. (May no such storm
Fall on our times, when ruin must reform!)
Tell me, my Muse! what monstrous dire offence,

What crime could any Christian king incense
To such a rage? Was't luxury, or lust?
Was he so temperate, so chaste, so just?
Were these their crimes? They were his own much more;
But wealth is crime enough to him that's poor,
Who having spent the treasures of his crown,
Condemns their luxury to feed his own.
And yet this act, to varnish o'er the shame
Of sacrilege, must bear devotion's name.
No crime so bold, but would be understood
A real, or at least a seeming good:
Who fears not to do ill, yet fears the name,
And, free from conscience, is a slave to fame.
Thus he the church at once protects, and spoils:
But princes' swords are sharper than their styles;
And thus to th'ages past he makes amends,
Their charity destroys, their faith defends.
Then did Religion in a lazy cell,
In empty, airy contemplations dwell;
And like the block, unmovèd lay; but ours,
As much too active, like the stork devours.
Is there no temp'rate region can be known,
Betwixt their frigid, and our torrid zone?
Could we not wake from that lethargic dream,
But to be restless in a worse extreme?
And for that lethargy was there no cure,
But to be cast into a calenture?
Can knowledge have no bound, but must advance
So far, to make us wish for ignorance,
And rather in the dark to grope our way,
Than, led by a false guide, to err by day?
Who sees these dismal heaps, but would demand
What barbarous invader sack'd the land?
But when he hears no Goth, no Turk did bring
This desolation, but a Christian king;
When nothing but the name of zeal appears
'Twixt our best actions and the worst of theirs,
What does he think our sacrilege would spare,
When such th'effects of our devotions are?
Parting from thence 'twixt anger, shame and fear,
Those for what's past, and this for what's too near,
My eye descending from the hill, surveys
Where Thames among the wanton valleys strays.
Thames, the most loved of all the Ocean's sons
By his old sire, to his embraces runs;
Hasting to pay his tribute to the sea,
Like mortal life to meet eternity.
Though with those streams he no resemblance hold,

Whose foam is amber, and their gravel gold,
His genuine and less guilty wealth t'explore,
Search not his bottom, but survey his shore,
O'er which he kindly spreads his spacious wing,
And hatches plenty for th'ensuing spring;
Nor then destroys it with too fond a stay,
Like mothers which their infants overlay;
Nor with a sudden and impetuous wave,
Like profuse kings, resumes the wealth he gave.
No unexpected inundations spoil
The mower's hopes, nor mock the ploughman's toil:
But godlike his unwearied bounty flows;
First loves to do, then loves the good he does.
Nor are his blessings to his banks confined,
But free and common as the sea or wind;
When he, to boast or to disperse his stores,
Full of the tributes of his grateful shores,
Visits the world, and in his flying towers
Brings home to us, and makes both Indies ours;
Finds wealth where 'tis, bestows it where it wants,
Cities in deserts, woods in cities plants;
So that to us no thing, no place is strange,
While his fair bosom is the world's exchange.
Oh, could I flow like thee, and make thy stream
My great example, as it is my theme!
Though deep, yet clear; though gentle, yet not dull;
Strong without rage, without o'erflowing full.
Heaven her Eridanus no more shall boast,
Whose fame in thine, like lesser current, 's lost;
Thy nobler streams shall visit Jove's abodes,
To shine among the stars,[5] and bathe the gods.
Here Nature, whether more intent to please
Us or herself with strange varieties,
(For things of wonder give no less delight
To the wise maker's, than beholder's sight;
Though these delights from sev'ral causes move;
For so our children, thus our friends, we love),
Wisely she knew the harmony of things,
As well as that of sounds, from discord springs.
Such was the discord, which did first disperse
Form, order, beauty, through the universe;
While dryness moisture, coldness heat resists,
All that we have, and that we are, subsists;
While the steep, horrid roughness of the wood
Strives with the gentle calmness of the flood,
Such huge extremes when Nature doth unite,
Wonder from thence results, from thence delight.
The stream is so transparent, pure, and clear,

That had the self-enamour'd youth[6] gazed here,
So fatally deceived he had not been,
While he the bottom, not his face had seen.
But his proud head the airy mountain hides
Among the clouds; his shoulders and his sides
A shady mantle clothes; his curlèd brows
Frown on the gentle stream, which calmly flows,
While winds and storms his lofty forehead beat:
The common fate of all that's high or great.
Low at his foot a spacious plain is placed,
Between the mountain and the stream embraced,
Which shade and shelter from the hill derives,
While the kind river wealth and beauty gives,
And in the mixture of all these appears
Variety, which all the rest endears.
This scene had some bold Greek or British bard
Beheld of old, what stories had we heard
Of fairies, satyrs, and the nymphs their dames,
Their feasts, their revels, and their am'rous flames?
'Tis still the same, although their airy shape
All but a quick poetic sight escape.
There Faunus and Sylvanus keep their courts,
And thither all the horned host resorts
To graze the ranker mead; that noble herd
On whose sublime and shady fronts is rear'd
Nature's great masterpiece; to show how soon,
Great things are made, but sooner are undone.
Here have I seen the King, when great affairs
Gave leave to slacken, and unbend his cares,
Attended to the chase by all the flower
Of youth whose hopes a nobler prey devour:
Pleasure with praise and danger they would buy,
And wish a foe that would not only fly.
The stag now conscious of his fatal growth,
At once indulgent to his fear and sloth,
To some dark covert his retreat had made,
Where nor man's eye, nor heaven's should invade
His soft repose; when th'unexpected sound
Of dogs, and men, his wakeful ears does wound.
Roused with the noise, he scarce believes his ear,
Willing to think th'illusions of his fear
Had given this false alarm, but straight his view
Confirms that more than all he fears is true.
Betray'd in all his strengths, the wood beset;
All instruments, all arts of ruin met;
He calls to mind his strength and then his speed,
His winged heels, and then his armed head;
With these t'avoid, with that his fate to meet:

But fear prevails, and bids him trust his feet.
So fast he flies, that his reviewing eye
Has lost the chasers, and his ear the cry;
Exulting, till he finds their nobler sense
Their disproportion'd speed doth recompense;
Then curses his conspiring feet, whose scent
Betrays that safety which their swiftness lent;
Then tries his friends; among the baser herd,
Where he so lately was obey'd and fear'd,
His safety seeks; the herd, unkindly wise,
Or chases him from thence, or from him flies;
Like a declining statesman, left forlorn
To his friends' pity, and pursuers' scorn,
With shame remembers, while himself was one
Of the same herd, himself the same had done.
Thence to the coverts and the conscious groves,
The scenes of his past triumphs and his loves;
Sadly surveying where he ranged alone
Prince of the soil, and all the herd his own,
And like a bold knight-errant did proclaim.
Combat to all, and bore away the dame,
And taught the woods to echo to the stream
His dreadful challenge, and his clashing beam;
Yet faintly now declines the fatal strife;
So much his love was dearer than his life.
Now every leaf, and every moving breath
Presents a foe, and every foe a death.
Wearied, forsaken, and pursued, at last
All safety in despair of safety placed,
Courage he thence resumes, resolved to bear
All their assaults, since 'tis in vain to fear.
And now, too late, he wishes for the fight
That strength he wasted in ignoble flight:
But when he sees the eager chase renew'd,
Himself by dogs, the dogs by men pursued,
He straight revokes his bold resolve, and more
Repents his courage than his fear before;
Finds that uncertain ways unsafest are,
And doubt a greater mischief than despair.
Then to the stream, when neither friends, nor force,
Nor speed, nor art, avail, he shapes his course;
Thinks not their rage so desperate to assay
An element more merciless than they.
But fearless they pursue, nor can the flood
Quench their dire thirst; alas! they thirst for blood.
So t'wards a ship the oar-finn'd galleys ply,
Which, wanting sea to ride, or wind to fly,
Stands but to fall revenged on those that dare

Tempt the last fury of extreme despair.
So fares the stag, among th'enraged hounds,
Repels their force, and wounds returns for wounds;
And as a hero, whom his baser foes
In troops surround, now these assails, now those,
Though prodigal of life, disdains to die
By common hands; but if he can descry
Some nobler foe approach, to him he calls,
And begs his fate, and then contented falls.
So when the king a mortal shaft lets fly
From his unerring hand, then glad to die,
Proud of the wound, to it resigns his blood,
And stains the crystal with a purple flood.
This a more innocent, and happy chase,
Than when of old, but in the selfsame place,
Fair Liberty pursued,[7] and meant a prey
To lawless power, here turn'd, and stood at bay;
When in that remedy all hope was placed
Which was, or should have been at least, the last.
Here was that charter seal'd, wherein the crown
All marks of arbitrary power lays down:
Tyrant and slave, those names of hate and fear,
The happier style of king and subject bear:
Happy, when both to the same centre move,
When kings give liberty, and subjects love.
Therefore not long in force this charter stood;
Wanting that seal, it must be seal'd in blood.
The subjects arm'd, the more their princes gave,
Th' advantage only took the more to crave;
Till kings by giving, give themselves away,
And e'en that power, that should deny, betray.
'Who gives constrain'd, but his own fear reviles,
Not thank'd, but scorn'd; nor are they gifts, but spoils.'
Thus kings, by grasping more than they could hold,
First made their subjects, by oppression, bold:
And popular sway, by forcing kings to give
More than was fit for subjects to receive,
Ran to the same extremes; and one excess
Made both, by striving to be greater, less.
When a calm river, raised with sudden rains,
Or snows dissolved, o'erflows th'adjoining plains,
The husbandmen with high raised banks secure
Their greedy hopes, and this he can endure;
But if with bays and dams they strive to force
His channel to a new, or narrow course;
No longer then within his banks he dwells,
First to a torrent, then a deluge, swells;
Stronger and fiercer by restraint he roars,

And knows no bound, but makes his power his shores.

FOOTNOTES

[1] 'Such a Muse': Mr. Waller.
[2] 'Great Edward, and thy greater son': Edward III. and the Black   Prince.
[3] 'Thy Bellona': Queen Phillippa.
[4] 'Captive king': the kings of France and Scotland.
[5] 'The stars': the Forest.
[6] 'Self-enamour'd youth': Narcissus.
[7] 'Liberty pursued': Runimede, where Magna Charta was first sealed.

THE DESTRUCTION OF TROY

AN ESSAY ON THE SECOND BOOK OF VIRGIL'S AENEIS, WRITTEN IN THE YEAR 1636.

THE ARGUMENT

The first book speaks of Aeneas's voyage by sea, and how, being cast by tempest upon the coast of Carthage, he was received by Queen Dido, who, after the feast, desires him to make the relation of the destruction of Troy; which is the argument of this book.

While all with silence and attention wait,
Thus speaks Aeneas from the bed of state:—
Madam, when you command us to review
Our fate, you make our old wounds bleed anew,
And all those sorrows to my sense restore,
Whereof none saw so much, none suffer'd more.
Not the most cruel of our conqu'ring foes
So unconcern'dly can relate our woes,
As not to lend a tear; then how can I
Repress the horror of my thoughts, which fly
The sad remembrance? Now th'expiring night
And the declining stars to rest invite;
Yet since 'tis your command, what you so well
Are pleased to hear, I cannot grieve to tell.
By fate repell'd and with repulses tired,
The Greeks, so many lives and years expired,
A fabric like a moving mountain frame,
Pretending vows for their return; this Fame
Divulges; then within the beast's vast womb
The choice and flower of all their troops entomb;
In view the isle of Tenedos, once high,
In fame and wealth, while Troy remain'd, doth lie;
(Now but an unsecure and open bay)
Thither by stealth the Greeks their fleet convey.
We gave them gone,[1] and to Mycenæ sail'd,

And Troy reviv'd, her mourning face unveil'd;
All through th'unguarded gates with joy resort
To see the slighted camp, the vacant port;
Here lay Ulysses, there Achilles; here
The battles join'd; the Grecian fleet rode there;
But the vast pile th'amazèd vulgar views,
Till they their reason in their wonder lose.
And first Thymoetes moves (urged by the power
Of fate, or fraud) to place it in the tower;
But Capys and the graver sort thought fit
The Greeks' suspected present to commit
To seas or flames, at least to search and bore
The sides, and what that space contains, t'explore.
Th' uncertain multitude with both engaged,
Divided stands, till from the tower, enraged
Laocoon ran, whom all the crowd attends,
Crying, 'What desp'rate frenzy's this, O friends!
To think them gone? Judge rather their retreat
But a design; their gifts but a deceit;
For our destruction 'twas contrived no doubt,
Or from within by fraud, or from without
By force. Yet know ye not Ulysses' shifts?
Their swords less danger carry than their gifts.'
(This said) against the horse's side his spear
He throws, which trembles with enclosèd fear,
Whilst from the hollows of his womb proceed
Groans, not his own; and had not Fate decreed
Our ruin, we had fill'd with Grecian blood
The place; then Troy and Priam's throne had stood.
Meanwhile a fetter'd pris'ner to the king
With joyful shouts the Dardan shepherds bring,
Who to betray us did himself betray,
At once the taker, and at once the prey;
Firmly prepared, of one event secured,
Or of his death or his design assured.
The Trojan youth about the captive flock,
To wonder, or to pity, or to mock.
Now hear the Grecian fraud, and from this one
Conjecture all the rest.
Disarm'd, disorder'd, casting round his eyes
On all the troops that guarded him, he cries,
'What land, what sea, for me what fate attends?
Caught by my foes, condemned by my friends,
Incensèd Troy a wretched captive seeks
To sacrifice; a fugitive the Greeks.'—
To pity this complaint our former rage
Converts; we now inquire his parentage;
What of their counsels or affairs he knew

Then fearless he replies, 'Great king! to you
All truth I shall relate: nor first can I
Myself to be of Grecian birth deny;
And though my outward state misfortune hath
Depress'd thus low, it cannot reach my faith.
You may by chance have heard the famous name
Of Palamede, who from old Belus came,
Whom, but for voting peace, the Greeks pursue,
Accus'd unjustly, then unjustly slew,
Yet mourn'd his death. My father was his friend,
And me to his commands did recommend,
While laws and councils did his throne support;
I but a youth, yet some esteem and port
We then did bear, till by Ulysses' craft
(Things known I speak) he was of life bereft:
Since, in dark sorrow I my days did spend,
Till now, disdaining his unworthy end,
I could not silence my complaints, but vow'd
Revenge, if ever fate or chance allow'd
My wish'd return to Greece; from hence his hate,
From thence my crimes, and all my ills bear date:
Old guilt fresh malice gives; the people's ears
He fills with rumours, and their hearts with fears,
And then the prophet to his party drew.
But why do I those thankless truths pursue,
Or why defer your rage? on me, for all
The Greeks, let your revenging fury fall.
Ulysses this, th'Atridæ this desire
At any rate.'—We straight are set on fire
(Unpractised in such myst'ries) to inquire
The manner and the cause: which thus he told,
With gestures humble, as his tale was bold.
'Oft have the Greeks (the siege detesting) tired
With tedious war, a stolen retreat desired,
And would to Heaven they'd gone! but still dismay'd
By seas or skies, unwillingly they stay'd.
Chiefly when this stupendous pile was raised,
Strange noises filled the air; we, all amazed,
Despatch Eurypylus t'inquire our fates,
Who thus the sentence of the gods relates:
"A virgin's slaughter did the storm appease,
When first t'wards Troy the Grecians took the seas;
Their safe retreat another Grecian's blood
Must purchase." All at this confounded stood;
Each thinks himself the man, the fear on all
Of what the mischief but on one can fall.
Then Calchas (by Ulysses first inspired)
Was urged to name whom th'angry god required;

Yet was I warn'd (for many were as well
Inspired as he) and did my fate foretell.
Ten days the prophet in suspense remain'd,
Would no man's fate pronounce; at last constrain'd
By Ithacus, he solemnly design'd
Me for the sacrifice; the people join'd
In glad consent, and all their common fear
Determine in my fate. The day drew near,
The sacred rites prepared, my temples crown'd
With holy wreaths; then I confess I found
The means to my escape; my bonds I brake,
Fled from my guards, and in a muddy lake
Amongst the sedges all the night lay hid,
Till they their sails had hoist (if so they did).
And now, alas! no hope remains for me
My home, my father, and my sons to see,
Whom they, enraged, will kill for my offence,
And punish, for my guilt, their innocence.
Those gods who know the truths I now relate,
That faith which yet remains inviolate
By mortal men, by these I beg; redress
My causeless wrongs, and pity such distress.'—
And now true pity in exchange he finds
For his false tears, his tongue his hands unbinds.
Then spake the king, 'Be ours, whoe'er thou art;
Forget the Greeks. But first the truth impart,
Why did they raise, or to what use intend
This pile? to a warlike or religious end?'
Skilful in fraud (his native art) his hands
T'ward heaven he raised, deliver'd now from bands.
'Ye pure ethereal flames! ye powers adored
By mortal men! ye altars, and the sword
I 'scaped! ye sacred fillets that involved
My destined head! grant I may stand absolved
From all their laws and rights, renounce all name
Of faith or love, their secret thoughts proclaim;
Only, O Troy! preserve thy faith to me,
If what I shall relate preserveth thee.
From Pallas' favour all our hopes, and all
Counsels and actions took original,
Till Diomed (for such attempts made fit
By dire conjunction with Ulysses' wit)
Assails the sacred tower, the guards they slay,
Defile with bloody hands, and thence convey
The fatal image; straight with our success
Our hopes fell back, whilst prodigies express
Her just disdain, her flaming eyes did throw
Flashes of lightning, from each part did flow

A briny sweat; thrice brandishing her spear,
Her statue from the ground itself did rear;
Then, that we should our sacrilege restore,
And re-convey their gods from Argos' shore,
Calchas persuades, till then we urge in vain
The fate of Troy. To measure back the main
They all consent, but to return again,
When reinforced with aids of gods and men.
Thus Calchas; then instead of that, this pile
To Pallas was design'd; to reconcile
Th' offended power, and expiate our guilt;
To this vast height and monstrous stature built,
Lest through your gates received, it might renew
Your vows to her, and her defence to you.
But if this sacred gift you disesteem,
Then cruel plagues (which Heaven divert on them!)
Shall fall on Priam's state: but if the horse
Your walls ascend, assisted by your force,
A league 'gainst Greece all Asia shall contract;
Our sons then suff'ring what their sires would act.'

Thus by his fraud and our own faith o'ercome,
A feigned tear destroys us, against whom
Tydides nor Achilles could prevail,
Nor ten years' conflict, nor a thousand sail.
This seconded by a most sad portent,
Which credit to the first imposture lent;
Laocoon, Neptune's priest, upon the day
Devoted to that god, a bull did slay;
When two prodigious serpents were descried,
Whose circling strokes the sea's smooth face divide;
Above the deep they raise their scaly crests,
And stem the flood with their erected breasts,
Their winding tails advance and steer their course,
And 'gainst the shore the breaking billows force.
Now landing, from their brandish'd tongues there came
A dreadful hiss, and from their eyes a flame.
Amazed we fly, directly in a line
Laocoon they pursue, and first entwine
(Each preying upon one) his tender sons;
Then him, who armed to their rescue runs,
They seized, and with entangling folds embraced,
His neck twice compassing, and twice his waist:
Their pois'nous knots he strives to break and tear,
While slime and blood his sacred wreaths besmear;
Then loudly roars, as when th'enraged bull
From th'altar flies, and from his wounded skull
Shakes the huge axe; the conqu'ring serpents fly

To cruel Pallas' altar, and there lie
Under her feet, within her shield's extent.
We, in our fears, conclude this fate was sent
Justly on him, who struck the sacred oak
With his accursed lance. Then to invoke
The goddess, and let in the fatal horse,
We all consent.

A spacious breach we make, and Troy's proud wall
Built by the gods, by our own hands doth fall;
Thus, all their help to their own ruin give,
Some draw with cords, and some the monster drive
With rolls and levers: thus our works it climbs
Big with our fate; the youth with songs and rhymes,
Some dance, some hale the rope; at last let down
It enters with a thund'ring noise the town.
Oh Troy! the seat of gods, in war renown'd!
Three times it struck; as oft the clashing sound
Of arms was heard; yet blinded by the power
Of Fate, we place it in the sacred tower.
Cassandra then foretells th'event, but she
Finds no belief (such was the gods' decree).
The altars with fresh flowers we crown, and waste
In feasts that day, which was (alas!) our last.
Now by the revolution of the skies
Night's sable shadows from the ocean rise,
Which heaven and earth, and the Greek frauds involved,
The city in secure repose dissolved,
When from the admiral's high poop appears
A light, by which the Argive squadron steers
Their silent course to Ilium's well-known shore,
When Sinon (saved by the gods' partial power)
Opens the horse, and through the unlock'd doors
To the free air the armed freight restores:
Ulysses, Stheneleus, Tisander slide
Down by a rope, Machaon was their guide;
Atrides, Pyrrhus, Thoas, Athamas,
And Epeus who the fraud's contriver was.
The gates they seize; the guards, with sleep and wine
Oppress'd, surprise, and then their forces join.
'Twas then, when the first sweets of sleep repair
Our bodies spent with toil, our minds with care,
(The gods' best gift), when, bathed in tears and blood,
Before my face lamenting Hector stood,
His aspect such when, soil'd with bloody dust,
Dragg'd by the cords which through his feet were thrust
By his insulting foe; oh, how transform'd,
How much unlike that Hector, who return'd

Clad in Achilles' spoils! when he, among
A thousand ships (like Jove) his lightning flung!
His horrid beard and knotted tresses stood
Stiff with his gore, and all his wounds ran blood:
Entranced I lay, then (weeping) said, 'The joy,
The hope and stay of thy declining Troy!
What region held thee? whence, so much desired,
Art thou restored to us, consumed and tired
With toils and deaths? But what sad cause confounds
Thy once fair looks, or why appear those wounds?'
Regardless of my words, he no reply
Returns, but with a dreadful groan doth cry,
'Fly from the flame, O goddess-born! our walls
The Greeks possess, and Troy confounded falls
From all her glories; if it might have stood
By any power, by this right hand it should.
What man could do, by me for Troy was done.
Take here her relics and her gods, to run
With them thy fate, with them new walls expect,
Which, toss'd on seas, thou shalt at last erect;'—
Then brings old Vesta from her sacred choir,
Her holy wreaths, and her eternal fire.
Meanwhile the walls with doubtful cries resound
From far (for shady coverts did surround
My father's house); approaching still more near,
The clash of arms, and voice of men we hear:
Roused from my bed, I speedily ascend
The houses' tops, and listening there attend.
As flames roll'd by the winds' conspiring force,
O'er full-ear'd corn, or torrent's raging course
Bears down th'opposing oaks, the fields destroys,
And mocks the ploughman's toil, th'unlook'd for noise
From neighb'ring hills th'amazed shepherd hears;
Such my surprise, and such their rage appears.
First fell thy house, Ucalegon! then thine
Deïphobus! Sigæan seas did shine
Bright with Troy's flames; the trumpets' dreadful sound
The louder groans of dying men confound.
Give me my arms, I cried, resolved to throw
Myself 'mong any that opposed the foe:
Rage, anger, and despair at once suggest,
That of all deaths, to die in arms was best.
The first I met was Pantheus, Phoebus' priest,
Who, 'scaping with his gods and relics, fled,
And t'wards the shore his little grandchild led;
'Pantheus, what hope remains? what force, what place
Made good? But, sighing, he replies, 'Alas!
Trojans we were, and mighty Ilium was;

But the last period and the fatal hour
Of Troy is come: our glory and our power
Incensèd Jove transfers to Grecian hands;
The foe within the burning town commands;
And (like a smother'd fire) an unseen force
Breaks from the bowels of the fatal horse:
Insulting Sinon flings about the flame,
And thousands more than e'er from Argos came
Possess the gates, the passes, and the streets,
And these the sword o'ertakes, and those it meets.
The guard nor fights nor flies; their fate so near
At once suspends their courage and their fear.'—
Thus by the gods, and by Atrides' words
Inspir'd, I make my way through fire, through swords,
Where noises, tumults, outcries, and alarms
I heard; first Iphitus, renown'd for arms,
We meet, who knew us (for the moon did shine)
Then Ripheus, Hypanis, and Dymas join
Their force, and young Choroebus, Mygdon's son,
Who, by the love of fair Cassandra won,
Arrived but lately in her father's aid;
Unhappy, whom the threats could not dissuade
Of his prophetic spouse;
Whom when I saw, yet daring to maintain
The fight, I said, 'Brave spirits! (but in vain)
Are you resolv'd to follow one who dares
Tempt all extremes? The state of our affairs
You see: the gods have left us, by whose aid
Our empire stood; nor can the flame be stay'd:
Then let us fall amidst our foes; this one
Relief the vanquish'd have, to hope for none.'
Then reinforced, as in a stormy night
Wolves urgèd by their raging appetite
Forage for prey, which their neglected young
With greedy jaws expect, even so among
Foes, fire, and swords, t'assured death we pass;
Darkness our guide, Despair our leader was.
Who can relate that evening's woes and spoils,
Or can his tears proportion to our toils?
The city, which so long had flourish'd, falls;
Death triumphs o'er the houses, temples, walls.
Nor only on the Trojans fell this doom,
Their hearts at last the vanquish'd reassume;
And now the victors fall: on all sides fears,
Groans, and pale Death in all her shapes appears!
Androgeus first with his whole troop was cast
Upon us, with civility misplaced
Thus greeting us, 'You lose, by your delay,

Your share, both of the honour and the prey;
Others the spoils of burning Troy convey
Back to those ships which you but now forsake.'
We making no return, his sad mistake
Too late he finds; as when an unseen snake
A traveller's unwary foot hath press'd,
Who trembling starts, when the snake's azure crest,
Swoll'n with his rising anger, he espies,
So from our view surprised Androgeus flies.
But here an easy victory we meet:
Fear binds their hands and ignorance their feet.
Whilst fortune our first enterprise did aid,
Encouraged with success, Choroebus said,
'O friends! we now by better fates are led,
And the fair path they lead us, let us tread.
First change your arms, and their distinctions bear;
The same, in foes, deceit and virtue are.'
Then of his arms Androgeus he divests,
His sword, his shield he takes, and plumèd crests;
Then Ripheus, Dymas, and the rest, all glad
Of the occasion, in fresh spoils are clad.
Thus mix'd with Greeks, as if their fortune still
Follow'd their swords, we fight, pursue, and kill.
Some re-ascend the horse, and he whose sides
Let forth the valiant, now the coward hides.
Some to their safer guard, their ships, retire;
But vain's that hope 'gainst which the gods conspire;
Behold the royal virgin, the divine
Cassandra, from Minerva's fatal shrine
Dragg'd by the hair, casting t'wards heaven, in vain,
Her eyes; for cords her tender hands did strain;
Choroebus at the spectacle enraged,
Flies in amidst the foes: we thus engaged,
To second him, among the thickest ran;
Here first our ruin from our friends began,
Who from the temple's battlements a shower
Of darts and arrows on our heads did pour:
They us for Greeks, and now the Greeks (who knew
Cassandra's rescue) us for Trojans slew.
Then from all parts Ulysses, Ajax then,
And then th'Atridæ rally all their men;
As winds, that meet from sev'ral coasts, contest,
Their prisons being broke, the south and west,
And Eurus on his winged coursers borne,
Triumphing in their speed, the woods are torn,
And chasing Nereus with his trident throws
The billows from their bottom; then all those
Who in the dark our fury did escape,

Returning, know our borrow'd arms and shape,
And diff'ring dialect: then their numbers swell
And grow upon us; first Choroebus fell
Before Minerva's altar, next did bleed
Just Ripheus, whom no Trojan did exceed
In virtue, yet the gods his fate decreed.
Then Hypanis and Dymas, wounded by
Their friends; nor thee, Pantheus! thy piety,
Nor consecrated mitre, from the same
Ill fate could save. My country's fun'ral flame
And Troy's cold ashes I attest, and call
To witness for myself, that in their fall
No foes, no death, nor danger I declin'd,
Did, and deserv'd no less, my fate to find.
Now Iphitus with me, and Pelias
Slowly retire; the one retarded was
By feeble age, the other by a wound;
To court the cry directs us, where we found
Th' assault so hot, as if 'twere only there,
And all the rest secure from foes or fear:
The Greeks the gates approach'd, their targets cast
Over their heads; some scaling ladders placed
Against the walls, the rest the steps ascend,
And with their shields on their left arms defend
Arrows and darts, and with their right hold fast
The battlement; on them the Trojans cast
Stones, rafters, pillars, beams; such arms as these,
Now hopeless, for their last defence they seize.
The gilded roofs, the marks of ancient state,
They tumble down; and now against the gate
Of th'inner court their growing force they bring;
Now was our last effort to save the king,
Relieve the fainting, and succeed the dead.
A private gallery 'twixt th'apartments led,
Not to the foe yet known, or not observed,
(The way for Hector's hapless wife reserved,
When to the aged king her little son
She would present); through this we pass, and run
Up to the highest battlement, from whence
The Trojans threw their darts without offence,
A tower so high, it seem'd to reach the sky,
Stood on the roof, from whence we could descry,
All Ilium—both the camps, the Grecian fleet;
This, where the beams upon the columns meet,
We loosen, which like thunder from the cloud
Breaks on their heads, as sudden and as loud.
But others still succeed: meantime, nor stones
Nor any kind of weapons cease.

Before the gate in gilded armour shone
Young Pyrrhus, like a snake, his skin new grown,
Who, fed on pois'nous herbs, all winter lay
Under the ground, and now reviews the day,
Fresh in his new apparel, proud and young,
Rolls up his back, and brandishes his tongue,
And lifts his scaly breast against the sun;
With him his father's squire, Automedon,
And Peripas who drove his winged steeds,
Enter the court; whom all the youth succeeds
Of Scyros' isle, who naming firebrands flung
Up to the roof; Pyrrhus himself among
The foremost with an axe an entrance hews
Through beams of solid oak, then freely views
The chambers, galleries, and rooms of state,
Where Priam and the ancient monarchs sate.
At the first gate an armed guard appears;
But th'inner court with horror, noise and tears,
Confus'dly fill'd, the women's shrieks and cries
The arched vaults re-echo to the skies;
Sad matrons wand'ring through the spacious rooms
Embrace and kiss the posts; then Pyrrhus comes;
Full of his father, neither men nor walls
His force sustain; the torn portcullis falls;
Then from the hinge their strokes the gates divorce,
And where the way they cannot find, they force.
Not with such rage a swelling torrent flows
Above his banks, th'opposing dams o'erthrows,
Depopulates the fields, the cattle, sheep,
Shepherds and folds, the foaming surges sweep.
And now between two sad extremes I stood,
Here Pyrrhus and th'Atridæ drunk with blood,
There th'hapless queen amongst an hundred dames,
And Priam quenching from his wounds those flames
Which his own hands had on the altar laid;
Then they the secret cabinets invade,
Where stood the fifty nuptial beds, the hopes
Of that great race; the golden posts, whose tops
Old hostile spoils adorn'd, demolished lay,
Or to the foe, or to the fire a prey.
Now Priam's fate perhaps you may inquire:
Seeing his empire lost, his Troy on fire,
And his own palace by the Greeks possess'd,
Arms long disused his trembling limbs invest;
Thus on his foes he throws himself alone,
Not for their fate, but to provoke his own:
There stood an altar open to the view
Of heaven, near which an aged laurel grew,

Whose shady arms the household gods embraced,
Before whose feet the queen herself had cast
With all her daughters, and the Trojan wives,
As doves whom an approaching tempest drives
And frights into one flock; but having spied
Old Priam clad in youthful arms, she cried,
'Alas! my wretched husband! what pretence
To bear those arms? and in them what defence?
Such aid such times require not, when again
If Hector were alive, he lived in vain;
Or here we shall a sanctuary find,
Or as in life, we shall in death be join'd.'
Then, weeping, with kind force held and embraced,
And on the secret seat the king she placed.
Meanwhile Polites, one of Priam's sons,
Flying the rage of bloody Pyrrhus, runs
Through foes and swords, and ranges all the court
And empty galleries, amazed and hurt;
Pyrrhus pursues him, now o'ertakes, now kills,
And his last blood in Priam's presence spills.
The king (though him so many deaths enclose)
Nor fear, nor grief, but indignation shows;
'The gods requite thee (if within the care
Of those above th'affairs of mortals are),
Whose fury on the son but lost had been,
Had not his parents' eyes his murder seen:
Not that Achilles (whom thou feign'st to be
Thy father) so inhuman was to me;
He blush'd, when I the rights of arms implored;
To me my Hector, me to Troy, restored.'
This said, his feeble arm a jav'lin flung,
Which on the sounding shield, scarce ent'ring, rung.
Then Pyrrhus; 'Go a messenger to hell
Of my black deeds, and to my father tell
The acts of his degen'rate race.' So through
His son's warm blood the trembling king he drew
To th'altar; in his hair one hand he wreathes;
His sword the other in his bosom sheaths.
Thus fell the king, who yet surviv'd the state,
With such a signal and peculiar fate,
Under so vast a ruin, not a grave,
Nor in such flames a fun'ral fire to have:
He whom such titles swell'd, such power made proud,
To whom the sceptres of all Asia bow'd,
On the cold earth lies th'unregarded king,
A headless carcase, and a nameless thing.

FOOTNOTE

ON THE EARL OF STRAFFORD'S TRIAL AND DEATH

Great Strafford! worthy of that name, though all
Of thee could be forgotten, but thy fall,
Crush'd by imaginary treason's weight,
Which too much merit did accumulate.
As chemists gold from brass by fire would draw,
Pretexts are into treason forged by law.
His wisdom such, at once it did appear
Three kingdoms' wonder, and three kingdoms' fear;
Whilst single he stood forth, and seem'd, although
Each had an army, as an equal foe.
Such was his force of eloquence, to make
The hearers more concern'd than he that spake;
Each seem'd to act that part he came to see,
And none was more a looker-on than he;
So did he move our passions, some were known
To wish, for the defence, the crime their own.
Now private pity strove with public hate,
Reason with rage, and eloquence with fate:
Now they could him, if he could them, forgive;
He's not too guilty, but too wise, to live:
Less seem those facts which treason's nickname bore,
Than such a fear'd ability for more.
They after death their fears of him express,
His innocence and their own guilt confess.
Their legislative frenzy they repent,
Enacting it should make no precedent.
This fate he could have 'scaped, but would not lose
Honour for life, but rather nobly chose
Death from their fears, than safety from his own,
That his last action all the rest might crown.

ON MY LORD CROFT'S AND MY JOURNEY INTO POLAND, FROM WHENCE WE BROUGHT £10,000 FOR HIS MAJESTY, BY THE DECIMATION OF HIS SCOTTISH SUBJECTS THERE

I
Toll, toll,
Gentle bell, for the soul
Of the pure ones in Pole,
Which are damn'd in our scroll.

II
Who having felt a touch
Of Cockram's greedy clutch,
Which though it was not much,
Yet their stubbornness was such,

III
That when we did arrive,
'Gainst the stream we did strive;
They would neither lead nor drive;

IV
Nor lend
An ear to a friend,
Nor an answer would send
To our letter so well penn'd;

V
Nor assist our affairs
With their moneys nor their wares,
As their answer now declares,
But only with their prayers.

VI
Thus they did persist
Did and said what they list,
'Till the Diet was dismiss'd;
But then our breech they kiss'd.

VII
For when
It was moved there and then,
They should pay one in ten,
The Diet said, Amen.

VIII
And because they are both
To discover the troth,
They must give word and oath,
Though they will forfeit both.

IX
Thus the constitution
Condemns them every one,
From the father to the son.

X
But John

(Our friend) Mollesson
Thought us to have outgone
With a quaint invention.

XI
Like the prophets of yore,
He complain'd long before,
Of the mischiefs in store,
Ay, and thrice as much more;

XII
And with that wicked lie,
A letter they came by
From our King's majesty.

XIII
But fate
Brought the letter too late,
'Twas of too old a date
To relieve their damn'd state.

XIV
The letter's to be seen,
With seal of wax so green,
At Dantzig, where 't has been
Turn'd into good Latin.

XV
But he that gave the hint,
This letter for to print,
Must also pay his stint.

XVI
That trick,
Had it come in the nick,
Had touch'd us to the quick;
But the messenger fell sick.

XVII
Had it later been wrote,
And sooner been brought,
They had got what they sought;
But now it serves for nought.

XVIII
On Sandys they ran aground,
And our return was crown'd
With full ten thousand pound.

I
Our resident Tom,
From Venice is come,
And hath left the statesman behind him;
Talks at the same pitch,
Is as wise, is as rich;
And just where you left him, you find him.

II
But who says he was not
A man of much plot,
May repent that false accusation;
Having plotted and penn'd
Six plays, to attend
The farce of his negotiation.

III
Before you were told
How Satan[1] the old
Came here with a beard to his middle;
Though he changed face and name,
Old Will was the same,
At the noise of a can and a fiddle.

IV
These statesmen, you believe,
Send straight for the shrieve,
For he is one too, or would be;
But he drinks no wine,
Which is a shrewd sign
That all's not so well as it should be.

V
These three, when they drink,
How little do they think
Of banishment, debts, or dying?
Not old with their years,
Nor cold with their fears;
But their angry stars still defying.

VI
Mirth makes them not mad,
Nor sobriety sad;

But of that they are seldom in danger;
At Paris, at Rome,
At the Hague, they're at home;
The good fellow is no where a stranger.

FOOTNOTE

[1] 'Satan': Mr. W. Murrey.

TO SIR JOHN MENNIS, BEING INVITED FROM CALAIS TO BOULOGNE, TO EAT A PIG

I
All on a weeping Monday,
With a fat vulgarian sloven,
Little admiral John
To Boulogne is gone,
Whom I think they call old Loven.

II
Hadst thou not thy fill of carting,[1]
Will Aubrey, Count of Oxon,
When nose lay in breech,
And breech made a speech,
So often cried, A pox on?

III
A knight by land and water
Esteem'd at such a high rate,
When 'tis told in Kent,
In a cart that he went,
They'll say now, Hang him, pirate.

IV
Thou might'st have ta'en example
From what thou read'st in story;
Being as worthy to sit
On an ambling tit
As thy predecessor Dory.

V
But, oh, the roof of linen,
Intended for a shelter!
But the rain made an ass
Of tilt and canvas,
And the snow, which you know is a melter.

VI

But with thee to inveigle
That tender stripling Astcot,
Who was soak'd to the skin,
Through drugget so thin,
Having neither coat nor waistcoat.

VII
He being proudly mounted,
Clad in cloak of Plymouth,
Defied cart so base,
For thief without grace,
That goes to make a wry mouth.

VIII
Nor did he like the omen,
For fear it might be his doom
One day for to sing,
With gullet in string,
A hymn of Robert Wisdom.

IX
But what was all this business?
For sure it was important;
For who rides i' th'wet
When affairs are not great,
The neighbours make but a sport on't.

X
To a goodly fat sow's baby,
O John! thou hadst a malice;
The old driver of swine
That day sure was thine,
Or thou hadst not quitted Calais.

FOOTNOTE
[1] 'Fill of carting': we three riding in a cart from Dunkirk to Calais, with a fat Dutch woman.

NATURA NATURATA

I
What gives us that fantastic fit,
That all our judgment and our wit
To vulgar custom we submit?

II
Treason, theft, murder, and all the rest

Of that foul legion we so detest,
Are in their proper names express'd.

III
Why is it then thought sin or shame
Those necessary parts to name,
From whence we went, and whence we came?

IV
Nature, whate'er she wants, requires;
With love inflaming our desires,
Finds engines fit to quench those fires.

V
Death she abhors; yet when men die
We are present; but no stander by
Looks on when we that loss supply.

VI
Forbidden wares sell twice as dear;
Even sack, prohibited last year,
A most abominable rate did bear.

VII
'Tis plain our eyes and ears are nice,
Only to raise, by that device,
Of those commodities the price.

VIII
Thus reason's shadows us betray,
By tropes and figures led astray,
From Nature, both her guide and way.

SARPEDON'S SPEECH TO GLAUCUS, IN THE TWELFTH BOOK OF HOMER

Thus to Glaucus spake
Divine Sarpedon, since he did not find
Others, as great in place, as great in mind:—
Above the rest why is our pomp, our power?
Our flocks, our herds, and our possessions more?
Why all the tributes land and sea affords
Heap'd in great chargers, load our sumptuous boards?
Our cheerful guests carouse the sparkling tears
Of the rich grape, while music charms their ears?
Why, as we pass, do those on Xanthus' shore,
As gods behold us, and as gods adore?

But that, as well in danger as degree,
We stand the first; that when our Licians see
Our brave examples, they admiring say,
Behold our gallant leaders! These are they
Deserve the greatness, and unenvied stand,
Since what they act transcends what they command.
Could the declining of this fate (O friend!)
Our date to immortality extend?
Or if death sought not them who seek not death,
Would I advance? or should my vainer breath
With such a glorious folly thee inspire?
But since with Fortune Nature doth conspire,
Since age, disease, or some less noble end,
Though not less certain, does our days attend;
Since 'tis decreed, and to this period lead
A thousand ways, the noblest path we'll tread,
And bravely on, till they, or we, or all,
A common sacrifice to honour fall.

FRIENDSHIP AND SINGLE LIFE, AGAINST LOVE AND MARRIAGE

I
Love! in what poison is thy dart
Dipp'd, when it makes a bleeding heart?
None know but they who feel the smart.

II
It is not thou, but we are blind,
And our corporeal eyes (we find)
Dazzle the optics of our mind.

III
Love to our citadel resorts;
Through those deceitful sally-ports,
Our sentinels betrays our forts.

IV
What subtle witchcraft man constrains,
To change his pleasure into pains,
And all his freedom into chains?

V
May not a prison, or a grave,
Like wedlock, honour's title have
That word makes freeborn man a slave.

VI

How happy he that loves not, lives!
Him neither hope nor fear deceives,
To Fortune who no hostage gives.

VII

How unconcern'd in things to come!
If here uneasy, finds at Rome,
At Paris, or Madrid, his home.

VIII

Secure from low and private ends,
His life, his zeal, his wealth attends
His prince, his country, and his friends.

IX

Danger and honour are his joy;
But a fond wife, or wanton boy,
May all those gen'rous thoughts destroy.

X

Then he lays by the public care;
Thinks of providing for an heir;
Learns how to get, and how to spare.

XI

Nor fire, nor foe, nor fate, nor night,
The Trojan hero did affright,
Who bravely twice renew'd the fight.

XII

Though still his foes in number grew,
Thicker their darts and arrows flew,
Yet, left alone, no fear he knew.

XIII

But Death in all her forms appears,
From every thing he sees and hears,
For whom he leads, and whom he bears.[1]

XIV

Love, making all things else his foes,
Like a fierce torrent, overflows
Whatever doth his course oppose.

XV

This was the cause, the poets sung,
Thy mother from the sea was sprung;

But they were mad to make thee young.

XVI

Her father, not her son, art thou:
From our desires our actions grow;
And from the cause th'effect must flow.

XVII

Love is as old as place or time;
'Twas he the fatal tree did climb,
Grandsire of father Adam's crime.

XVIII

Well may'st thou keep this world in awe;
Religion, wisdom, honour, law,
The tyrant in his triumph draw.

XIX

'Tis he commands the powers above;
Phoebus resigns his darts, and Jove
His thunder to the god of Love.

XX

To him doth his feign'd mother yield;
Nor Mars (her champion's) flaming shield
Guards him, when Cupid takes the field.

XXI

He clips Hope's wings, whose airy bliss
Much higher than fruition is,
But less than nothing if it miss.

XXII

When matches Love alone projects,
The cause transcending the effects,
That wild fire's quench'd in cold neglects;

XXIII

Whilst those conjunctions prove the best,
Where Love's of blindness dispossess'd
By perspectives of interest.

XXIV

Though Sol'mon with a thousand wives,
To get a wise successor strives,
But one (and he a fool) survives.

XXV

Old Rome of children took no care;
They with their friends their beds did share,
Secure t'adopt a hopeful heir.

XXVI

Love drowsy days and stormy nights
Makes; and breaks friendship, whose delights
Feed, but not glut our appetites.

XXVII

Well-chosen friendship, the most noble
Of virtues, all our joys makes double,
And into halves divides our trouble.

XXVIII

But when th'unlucky knot we tie,
Care, av'rice, fear, and jealousy
Make friendship languish till it die.

XXIX

The wolf, the lion, and the bear,
When they their prey in pieces tear,
To quarrel with themselves forbear;

XXX

Yet tim'rous deer, and harmless sheep,
When love into their veins doth creep,
That law of Nature cease to keep.

XXXI

Who, then, can blame the am'rous boy,
Who, the fair Helen to enjoy,
To quench his own, set fire on Troy?

XXXII

Such is the world's prepost'rous fate,
Amongst all creatures, mortal hate
Love (though immortal) doth create.

XXXIII

But love may beasts excuse, for they
Their actions not by reason sway,
But their brute appetites obey.

XXXIV

But man's that savage beast, whose mind
From reason to self-love declined,
Delights to prey upon his kind.

ON MR ABRAHAM COWLEY, HIS DEATH, AND BURIAL AMONGST THE ANCIENT POETS

Old Chaucer, like the morning star,
To us discovers day from far;
His light those mists and clouds dissolved,
Which our dark nation long involved:
But he descending to the shades,
Darkness again the age invades.
Next (like Aurora) Spenser rose,
Whose purple blush the day foreshows;
The other three with his own fires
Phoebus, the poet's god, inspires;
By Shakespeare's, Jonson's, Fletcher's lines,
Our stage's lustre Rome's outshines:
These poets near our princes sleep,
And in one grave their mansion keep.
They lived to see so many days,
Till time had blasted all their bays:
But cursèd be the fatal hour,
That pluck'd the fairest, sweetest flower
That in the Muses' garden grew,
And amongst wither'd laurels threw!
Time, which made them their fame outlive,
To Cowley scarce did ripeness give.
Old mother Wit, and Nature, gave
Shakespeare and Fletcher all they have;
In Spenser, and in Jonson, Art
Of slower Nature got the start;
But both in him so equal are,
None knows which bears the happiest share;
To him no author was unknown,
Yet what he wrote was all his own;
He melted not the ancient gold,
Nor, with Ben Jonson, did make bold
To plunder all the Roman stores
Of poets, and of orators:
Horace's wit, and Virgil's state,
He did not steal, but emulate!
And when he would like them appear,
Their garb, but not their clothes, did wear;
He not from Rome alone, but Greece,
Like Jason, brought the golden fleece;

To him that language (though to none
Of th'others) as his own was known.
On a stiff gale (as Flaccus[1] sings)
The Theban swan extends his wings,
When through th'ethereal clouds he flies;
To the same pitch our swan doth rise;
Old Pindar's flights by him are reach'd,
When on that gale his wings are stretch'd;
His fancy and his judgment such,
Each to the others seem'd too much,
His severe judgment (giving law)
His modest fancy kept in awe:
As rigid husbands jealous are,
When they believe their wives too fair.
His English streams so pure did flow
As all that saw and tasted know;
But for his Latin vein, so clear,
Strong,[2] full, and high it doth appear,
That were immortal Virgil here,
Him, for his judge, he would not fear;
Of that great portraiture so true
A copy pencil never drew.
My Muse her song had ended here,
But both their Genii straight appear,
Joy and amazement her did strike:
Two twins she never saw so like.
'Twas taught by wise Pythagoras,
One soul might through more bodies pass.
Seeing such transmigration there,
She thought it not a fable here.
Such a resemblance of all parts,
Life, death, age, fortune, nature, arts;
Then lights her torch at theirs, to tell,
And show the world this parallel:
Fix'd and contemplative their looks,
Still turning over Nature's books;
Their works chaste, moral and divine,
Where profit and delight combine;
They, gilding dirt, in noble verse
Rustic philosophy rehearse.
When heroes, gods, or god-like kings
They praise, on their exalted wings
To the celestial orbs they climb,
And with th'harmonious spheres keep time.
Nor did their actions fall behind
Their words, but with like candour sinned;
Each drew fair characters, yet none
Of these they feign'd, excels their own.

Both by two gen'rous princes loved,
Who knew, and judged what they approved;
Yet having each the same desire,
Both from the busy throng retire.
Their bodies, to their minds resign'd,
Cared not to propagate their kind:
Yet though both fell before their hour,
Time on their offspring hath no power,
Nor fire nor fate their bays shall blast,
Nor death's dark veil their day o'ercast.

FOOTNOTES
[1] 'Flaccus Horace': his Pindarics.
[2] 'Strong': his last works.

A SPEECH AGAINST PEACE AT THE CLOSE COMMITTEE

To the tune of, 'I went from England.'

I
But will you now to peace incline,
And languish in the main design,
And leave us in the lurch?
I would not monarchy destroy,
But as the only way t'enjoy
The ruin of the church.

II
Is not the Bishops' bill denied,
And we still threaten'd to be tried?
You see the King embraces
Those counsels he approved before:
Nor doth he promise, which is more,
That we shall have their places.

III
Did I for this bring in the Scot?
(For 'tis no secret now) the plot
Was Saye's and mine together;
Did I for this return again,
And spend a winter there in vain,
Once more t'invite them hither?

IV
Though more our money than our cause
Their brotherly assistance draws,

My labour was not lost.
At my return I brought you thence
Necessity, their strong pretence,
And these shall quit the cost.

V
Did I for this my country bring
To help their knight against their King,
And raise the first sedition?
Though I the business did decline,
Yet I contrived the whole design,
And sent them their petition.

VI
So many nights spent in the City
In that invisible Committee,
The wheel that governs all;
From thence the change in church and state,
And all the mischief bears the date
From Haberdashers' Hall.

VII
Did we force Ireland to despair,
Upon the King to cast the war,
To make the world abhor him,
Because the rebels used his name?
Though we ourselves can do the same,
While both alike were for him.

VIII
Then the same fire we kindled here
With what was given to quench it there,
And wisely lost that nation:
To do as crafty beggars use,
To maim themselves, thereby t'abuse
The simple man's compassion.

IX
Have I so often pass'd between
Windsor and Westminster, unseen,
And did myself divide:
To keep his Excellence in awe,
And give the Parliament the law?
For they knew none beside.

X
Did I for this take pains to teach
Our zealous ignorants to preach,

And did their lungs inspire;
Gave them their texts, show'd them their parts,
And taught them all their little arts,
To fling abroad the fire?

XI
Sometimes to beg, sometimes to threaten,
And say the Cavaliers are beaten,
To stroke the people's ears;
Then straight, when victory grows cheap,
And will no more advance the heap,
To raise the price of fears.

XII
And now the books, and now the bells,
And now our act, the preacher tells,
To edify the people;
All our divinity is news,
And we have made of equal use
The pulpit and the steeple.

XIII
And shall we kindle all this flame
Only to put it out again,
And must we now give o'er,
And only end where we begun?
In vain this mischief we have done,
If we can do no more.

XIV
If men in peace can have their right,
Where's the necessity to fight,
That breaks both law and oath?
They'll say they fight not for the cause,
Nor to defend the King and laws,
But us against them both.

XV
Either the cause at first was ill,
Or, being good, it is so still;
And thence they will infer,
That either now or at the first
They were deceived; or, which is worst,
That we ourselves may err.

XVI
But plague and famine will come in,
For they and we are near of kin,

And cannot go asunder:
But while the wicked starve, indeed
The saints have ready at their need
God's providence, and plunder.

XVII
Princes we are if we prevail,
And gallant villains if we fail.
When to our fame 'tis told,
It will not be our least of praise,
Since a new state we could not raise,
To have destroy'd the old.

XVIII
Then let us stay and fight, and vote,
Till London is not worth a groat;
Oh! 'tis a patient beast!
When we have gall'd and tired the mule,
And can no longer have the rule,
We'll have the spoil at least.

TO THE FIVE MEMBERS OF THE HONOURABLE HOUSE OF COMMONS, THE HUMBLE PETITION OF THE POETS

After so many concurring petitions
From all ages and sexes, and all conditions,
We come in the rear to present our follies
To Pym, Stroud, Haslerig, Hampden, and Hollis.
Though set form of prayer be an abomination,
Set forms of petitions find great approbation;
Therefore, as others from th'bottom of their souls,
So we from the depth and bottom of our bowels,
According unto the bless'd form you have taught us,
We thank you first for the ills you have brought us:
For the good we receive we thank him that gave it,
And you for the confidence only to crave it.
Next in course, we complain of the great violation
Of privilege (like the rest of our nation),
But 'tis none of yours of which we have spoken,
Which never had being until they were broken;
But ours is a privilege ancient and native,
Hangs not on an ord'nance, or power legislative.
And, first, 'tis to speak whatever we please,
Without fear of a prison or pursuivants' fees.
Next, that we only may lie by authority;
But in that also you have got the priority.

Next, an old custom, our fathers did name it
Poetical license, and always did claim it.
By this we have power to change age into youth,
Turn nonsense to sense, and falsehood to truth;
In brief, to make good whatsoever is faulty;
This art some poet, or the devil, has taught ye:
And this our property you have invaded,
And a privilege of both Houses have made it.
But that trust above all in poets reposed,
That kings by them only are made and deposed,
This though you cannot do, yet you are willing:
But when we undertake deposing or killing,
They're tyrants and monsters; and yet then the poet
Takes full revenge on the villains that do it:
And when we resume a sceptre or crown,
We are modest, and seek not to make it our own.
But is't not presumption to write verses to you,
Who make better poems by far of the two?
For all those pretty knacks you compose,
Alas! what are they but poems in prose?
And between those and ours there's no difference,
But that yours want the rhyme, the wit, and the sense:
But for lying (the most noble part of a poet)
You have it abundantly, and yourselves know it;
And though you are modest and seem to abhor it,
'T has done you good service, and thank Hell for it:
Although the old maxim remains still in force,
That a sanctified cause must have a sanctified course,
If poverty be a part of our trade,
So far the whole kingdom poets you have made,
Nay, even so far as undoing will do it,
You have made King Charles himself a poet:
But provoke not his Muse, for all the world knows,
Already you have had too much of his prose.

A WESTERN WONDER

I
Do you not know, not a fortnight ago,
How they bragg'd of a Western Wonder?
When a hundred and ten slew five thousand men,
With the help of lightning and thunder?

II
There Hopton was slain, again and again,
Or else my author did lie;

With a new thanksgiving, for the dead who are living,
To God, and his servant Chidleigh.

III
But now on which side was the miracle tried?
I hope we at last are even;
For Sir Ralph and his knaves are risen from their graves,
To cudgel the clowns of Devon.

IV
And there Stamford came, for his honour was lame
Of the gout three months together;
But it proved, when they fought, but a running gout,
For his heels were lighter than ever.

V
For now he outruns his arms and his guns,
And leaves all his money behind him;
But they follow after; unless he take water,
At Plymouth again they will find him.

VI
What Reading hath cost, and Stamford hath lost,
Goes deep in the sequestrations;
These wounds will not heal, with your new great seal,
Nor Jephson's declarations.

VII
Now, Peters and Case, in your prayer and grace,
Remember the new thanksgiving;
Isaac and his wife, now dig for your life,
Or shortly you'll dig for your living.

A SECOND WESTERN WONDER

I
You heard of that wonder, of the lightning and thunder,
Which made the lie so much the louder:
Now list to another, that miracle's brother,
Which was done with a firkin of powder.

II
Oh, what a damp it struck through the camp!
But as for honest Sir Ralph,
It blew him to the Vies without beard or eyes,
But at least three heads and a half.

III

When out came the book, which the newsmonger took,
From the preaching lady's letter,
Where in the first place, stood the conqueror's face,
Which made it show much the better.

IV

But now, without lying, you may paint him flying,
At Bristol they say you may find him,
Great William the Con, so fast did he run,
That he left half his name behind him.

V

And now came the post, save all that was lost,
But, alas! we are past deceiving
By a trick so stale, or else such a tale
Might amount to a new thanksgiving.

VI

This made Mr. Case, with a pitiful face,
In the pulpit to fall a weeping,
Though his mouth utter'd lies, truth fell from his eyes,
Which kept the Lord Mayor from sleeping.

VII

Now shut up shops, and spend your last drops,
For the laws, not your cause, you that loathe 'em,
Lest Essex should start, and play the second part
Of worshipful Sir John Hotham.

A SONG.

I

Morpheus! the humble god, that dwells
In cottages and smoky cells,
Hates gilded roofs and beds of down;
And though he fears no prince's frown,
Flies from the circle of a crown:

II

Come, I say, thou powerful god,
And thy leaden charming rod,
Dipp'd in the Lethean lake,
O'er his wakeful temples shake,
Lest he should sleep, and never wake.

III

Nature, (alas!) why art thou so
Obligèd to thy greatest foe?
Sleep that is thy best repast,
Yet of death it bears a taste,
And both are the same thing at last.

ON MR JOHN FLETCHER'S WORKS

So shall we joy, when all whom beasts and worms
Have turn'd to their own substances and forms:
Whom earth to earth, or fire hath changed to fire,
We shall behold more than at first entire;
As now we do to see all thine thy own
In this my Muse's resurrection,
Whose scatter'd parts from thy own race more wounds
Hath suffer'd than Actæon from his hounds;
Which first their brains, and then their belly fed,
And from their excrements new poets bred.
But now thy Muse enragèd, from her urn,
Like ghosts of murder'd bodies, does return
T' accuse the murderers, to right the stage,
And undeceive the long-abusèd age,
Which casts thy praise on them, to whom thy wit
Gives not more gold than they give dross to it;
Who not content, like felons, to purloin,
Add treason to it, and debase the coin.
But whither am I stray'd? I need not raise
Trophies to thee from other men's dispraise;
Nor is thy fame on lesser ruins built,
Nor needs thy juster title the foul guilt
Of eastern kings, who, to secure their reign,
Must have their brothers, sons, and kindred slain.
Then was wit's empire at the fatal height,
When labouring and sinking with its weight,
From thence a thousand lesser poets sprung,
Like petty princes from the fall of Rome;
When Jonson, Shakespeare, and thyself, did sit,
And sway'd in the triumvirate of wit.
Yet what from Jonson's oil and sweat did flow,
Or what more easy Nature did bestow
On Shakespeare's gentler Muse, in thee full grown
Their graces both appear, yet so that none
Can say, Here nature ends, and art begins;
But mix'd like th'elements, and born like twins,

So interwove, so like, so much the same,
None this mere nature, that mere art can name:
'Twas this the ancients meant; nature and skill
Are the two tops of their Parnassus' hill.

TO SIR RICHARD FANSHAW, UPON HIS TRANSLATION OF 'PASTOR FIDO.'

Such is our pride, our folly, or our fate,
That few but such as cannot write, translate.
But what in them is want of art or voice,
In thee is either modesty or choice.
While this great piece, restored by thee, doth stand
Free from the blemish of an artless hand,
Secure of fame, thou justly dost esteem
Less honour to create than to redeem.
Nor ought a genius less than his that writ
Attempt translation; for transplanted wit
All the defects of air and soil doth share,
And colder brains like colder climates are:
In vain they toil, since nothing can beget
A vital spirit but a vital heat.
That servile path thou nobly dost decline
Of tracing word by word, and line by line.
Those are the labour'd births of slavish brains,
Not the effect of poetry, but pains;
Cheap vulgar arts, whose narrowness affords
No flight for thoughts, but poorly sticks at words.
A new and nobler way thou dost pursue
To make translations and translators too.
They but preserve the ashes, thou the flame,
True to his sense, but truer to his fame:
Fording his current, where thou find'st it low,
Let'st in thine own to make it rise and flow;
Wisely restoring whatsoever grace
It lost by change of times, or tongues, or place.
Nor fetter'd to his numbers and his times,
Betray'st his music to unhappy rhymes.
Nor are the nerves of his compacted strength
Stretch'd and dissolved into unsinew'd length:
Yet, after all, (lest we should think it thine)
Thy spirit to his circle dost confine.
New names, new dressings, and the modern cast,
Some scenes, some persons alter'd, and outfaced
The world, it were thy work; for we have known
Some thank'd and praised for what was less their own.
That master's hand which to the life can trace

The airs, the lines, and features of the face,
May with a free and bolder stroke express
A varied posture, or a flatt'ring dress;
He could have made those like, who made the rest,
But that he knew his own design was best.

TO THE HON. EDWARD HOWARD, ON 'THE BRITISH PRINCES.'

What mighty gale hath raised a flight so strong,
So high above all vulgar eyes, so long?
One single rapture scarce itself confines
Within the limits of four thousand lines:
And yet I hope to see this noble heat
Continue till it makes the piece complete,
That to the latter age it may descend,
And to the end of time its beams extend.
When poesy joins profit with delight,
Her images should be most exquisite;
Since man to that perfection cannot rise,
Of always virtuous, fortunate, and wise;
Therefore the patterns man should imitate
Above the life our masters should create.
Herein if we consult with Greece and Rome,
Greece (as in war) by Rome was overcome;
Though mighty raptures we in Homer find,
Yet, like himself, his characters were blind:
Virgil's sublimèd eyes not only gazed,
But his sublimèd thoughts to heaven were raised.
Who reads the honours which he paid the gods
Would think he had beheld their bless'd abodes;
And that his hero might accomplish'd be,
From divine blood he draws his pedigree.
From that great judge your judgment takes its law,
And by the best original does draw
Bonduca's honour, with those heroes Time
Had in oblivion wrapp'd, his saucy crime:
To them and to your nation you are just,
In raising up their glories from the dust;
And to Old England you that right have done,
To show no story nobler than her own.

AN OCCASIONAL IMITATION OF A MODERN AUTHOR UPON THE GAME OF CHESS

A tablet stood of that abstersive tree,

Where Aethiop's swarthy bird did build her nest;
Inlaid it was with Libyan ivory,
Drawn from the jaws of Afric's prudent beast.
Two kings like Saul, much taller than the rest,
Their equal armies draw into the field;
Till one take th'other pris'ner they contest;
Courage and fortune must to conduct yield.
This game the Persian Magi did invent,
The force of Eastern wisdom to express;
From thence to busy Europeans sent,
And styled by modern Lombards pensive Chess.
Yet some that fled from Troy to Rome report,
Penthesilea Priam did oblige;
Her Amazons his Trojans taught this sport,
To pass the tedious hours of ten years' siege.
There she presents herself, whilst kings and peers
Look gravely on whilst fierce Bellona fights;
Yet maiden modesty her motions steers,
Nor rudely skips o'er bishops' heads like knights.

THE PASSION OF DIDO FOR AENEAS

Having at large declared Jove's embassy,
Cyllenius[1] from Aeneas straight doth fly;
He, loth to disobey the god's command,
Nor willing to forsake this pleasant land,
Ashamed the kind Eliza to deceive,
But more afraid to take a solemn leave,
He many ways his lab'ring thoughts revolves;
But fear o'ercoming shame, at last resolves
(Instructed by the god of thieves)[1] to steal
Himself away, and his escape conceal.
He calls his captains, bids them rig the fleet,
That at the port they privately should meet;
And some dissembled colour to project,
That Dido should not their design suspect;
But all in vain he did his plot disguise;
No art a watchful lover can surprise.
She the first motion finds; love though most sure,
Yet always to itself seems unsecure.
That wicked fame which their first love proclaim'd,
Foretells the end: the queen with rage inflamed,
Thus greets him: 'Thou dissembler! would'st thou fly
Out of my arms by stealth perfidiously?
Could not the hand I plighted, nor the love,
Nor thee the fate of dying Dido move?

And in the depth of winter, in the night,
Dark as thy black designs to take thy flight,
To plough the raging seas to coasts unknown,
The kingdom thou pretend'st to not thine own!
Were Troy restored, thou shouldst mistrust a wind
False as thy vows, and as thy heart unkind.
Fly'st thou from me? By these dear drops of brine
I thee adjure, by that right hand of thine,
By our espousals, by our marriage-bed,
If all my kindness ought have merited;
If ever I stood fair in thy esteem,
From ruin me and my lost house redeem.
Cannot my prayers a free acceptance find?
Nor my tears soften an obdurate mind?
My fame of chastity, by which the skies
I reached before, by thee extinguish'd dies.
Into my borders now Iarbas falls,
And my revengeful brother scales my walls;
The wild Numidians will advantage take;
For thee both Tyre and Carthage me forsake.
Hadst thou before thy flight but left with me
A young Aeneas who, resembling thee,
Might in my sight have sported, I had then
Not wholly lost, nor quite deserted been;
By thee, no more my husband, but my guest,
Betray'd to mischiefs, of which death's the least.'

With fixèd looks he stands, and in his breast
By Jove's command his struggling care suppress'd.
'Great queen! your favours and deserts so great,
Though numberless, I never shall forget;
No time, until myself I have forgot,
Out of my heart Eliza's name shall blot:
But my unwilling flight the gods enforce,
And that must justify our sad divorce.
Since I must you forsake, would Fate permit,
To my desires I might my fortune fit;
Troy to her ancient splendour I would raise,
And where I first began, would end my days.
But since the Lycian lots, and Delphic god
Have destined Italy for our abode;
Since you proud Carthage (fled from Tyre) enjoy,
Why should not Latium us receive from Troy?
As for my son, my father's angry ghost
Tells me his hopes by my delays are cross'd,
And mighty Jove's ambassador appear'd
With the same message, whom I saw and heard;
We both are grieved when you or I complain,

But much the more when all complaints are vain;
I call to witness all the gods, and thy
Beloved head, the coast of Italy
Against my will I seek.'

Whilst thus he speaks, she rolls her sparkling eyes,
Surveys him round, and thus incensed replies;
'Thy mother was no goddess, nor thy stock
From Dardanus, but in some horrid rock,
Perfidious wretch! rough Caucasus thee bred,
And with their milk Hyrcanian tigers fed.
Dissimulation I shall now forget,
And my reserves of rage in order set,
Could all my prayers and soft entreaties force
Sighs from his breast, or from his look remorse.
Where shall I first complain? can mighty Jove
Or Juno such impieties approve?
The just Astræa sure is fled to hell;
Nor more in earth, nor heaven itself will dwell.
Oh, Faith! him on my coasts by tempest cast,
Receiving madly, on my throne I placed;
His men from famine, and his fleet from fire
I rescued: now the Lycian lots conspire
With Phoebus; now Jove's envoy through the air
Brings dismal tidings; as if such low care
Could reach their thoughts, or their repose disturb!
Thou art a false impostor, and a fourbe;
Go, go, pursue thy kingdom through the main;
I hope, if Heaven her justice still retain,
Thou shalt be wreck'd, or cast upon some rock,
Where thou the name of Dido shalt invoke;
I'll follow thee in fun'ral flames; when dead
My ghost shall thee attend at board and bed,
And when the gods on thee their vengeance show,
That welcome news shall comfort me below.'

This saying, from his hated sight she fled;
Conducted by her damsels to her bed;
Yet restless she arose, and looking out,
Beholds the fleet, and hears the seamen shout
When great Aeneas pass'd before the guard,
To make a view how all things were prepared.
Ah, cruel Love! to what dost thou enforce
Poor mortal breasts! Again she hath recourse
To tears and prayers, again she feels the smart
Of a fresh wound from his tyrannic dart.
That she no ways nor means may leave untried,
Thus to her sister she herself applied:

'Dear sister, my resentment had not been
So moving, if this fate I had foreseen:
Therefore to me this last kind office do,
Thou hast some int'rest in our scornful foe;
He trusts to thee the counsels of his mind,
Thou his soft hours, and free access canst find;
Tell him I sent not to the Ilian coast
My fleet to aid the Greeks; his father's ghost
I never did disturb; ask him to lend
To this, the last request that I shall send,
A gentle ear; I wish that he may find
A happy passage, and a prosp'rous wind.
The contract I don't plead, which he betray'd,
Nor that his promised conquest be delay'd;
All that I ask is but a short reprieve,
Till I forget to love, and learn to grieve;
Some pause and respite only I require,
Till with my tears I shall have quench'd my fire.
If thy address can but obtain one day
Or two, my death that service shall repay.'
Thus she entreats; such messages with tears
Condoling Anne to him, and from him bears:
But him no prayers, no arguments can move;
The Fates resist, his ears are stopp'd by Jove.
As when fierce northern blasts from th'Alps descend,
From his firm roots with struggling gusts to rend
An aged sturdy oak, the rattling sound
Grows loud, with leaves and scatter'd arms the ground
Is overlaid; yet he stands fixed; as high
As his proud head is raised towards the sky,
So low t'wards hell his roots descend. With prayers
And tears the hero thus assail'd, great cares
He smothers in his breast, yet keeps his post,
All their addresses and their labour lost.
Then she deceives her sister with a smile:
'Anne, in the inner court erect a pile;
Thereon his arms and once-loved portrait lay,
Thither our fatal marriage-bed convey;
All cursèd monuments of him with fire
We must abolish (so the gods require).'
She gives her credit for no worse effect
Than from Sichæus' death she did suspect,
And her commands obeys.
Aurora now had left Tithonus' bed,
And o'er the world her blushing rays did spread;
The Queen beheld, as soon as day appear'd,
The navy under sail, the haven clear'd;
Thrice with her hand her naked breast she knocks,

And from her forehead tears her golden locks;
'O Jove!' she cried, 'and shall he thus delude
Me and my realm? why is he not pursued?
Arm, arm,' she cried, 'and let our Tyrians board
With ours his fleet, and carry fire and sword;
Leave nothing unattempted to destroy
That perjured race, then let us die with joy.
What if th'event of war uncertain were?
Nor death, nor danger, can the desp'rate fear.
But oh, too late! this thing I should have done,
When first I placed the traitor on my throne.
Behold the faith of him who saved from fire
His honour'd household gods, his aged sire
His pious shoulders from Troy's flames did bear;
Why did I not his carcase piecemeal tear,
And cast it in the sea? why not destroy
All his companions, and belovèd boy
Ascanius? and his tender limbs have dress'd,
And made the father on the son to feast?
Thou Sun! whose lustre all things here below
Surveys; and Juno! conscious of my woe;
Revengeful Furies! and Queen Hecate!
Receive and grant my prayer! If he the sea
Must needs escape, and reach th'Ausonian land,
If Jove decree it, Jove's decree must stand;
When landed, may he be with arms oppress'd
By his rebelling people, be distress'd
By exile from his country, be divorced
From young Ascanius' sight, and be enforced
To implore foreign aids, and lose his friends
By violent and undeservèd ends!
When to conditions of unequal peace
He shall submit, then may he not possess
Kingdom nor life, and find his funeral
I' th'sands, when he before his day shall fall!
And ye, O Tyrians! with immortal hate
Pursue this race, this service dedicate
To my deplorèd ashes; let there be
'Twixt us and them no league nor amity.
May from my bones a new Achilles rise,
That shall infest the Trojan colonies
With fire, and sword, and famine, when at length
Time to our great attempts contributes strength;
Our seas, our shores, our armies theirs oppose,
And may our children be for ever foes!'
A ghastly paleness death's approach portends,
Then trembling she the fatal pile ascends;
Viewing the Trojan relics, she unsheath'd

Aeneas' sword, not for that use bequeath'd:
Then on the guilty bed she gently lays
Herself, and softly thus lamenting prays;
'Dear relics! whilst that Gods and Fates give leave,
Free me from cares and my glad soul receive.
That date which Fortune gave, I now must end,
And to the shades a noble ghost descend.
Sichæus' blood, by his false brother spilt,
I have revenged, and a proud city built;
Happy, alas! too happy, I had lived,
Had not the Trojan on my coast arrived.
But shall I die without revenge? yet die
Thus, thus with joy to thy Sichæus fly.
My conscious foe my funeral fire shall view
From sea, and may that omen him pursue!'
Her fainting hand let fall the sword besmear'd
With blood, and then the mortal wound appear'd;
Through all the court the fright and clamours rise,
Which the whole city fills with fears and cries,
As loud as if her Carthage, or old Tyre
The foe had enter'd, and had set on fire.
Amazèd Anne with speed ascends the stairs,
And in her arms her dying sister rears;
'Did you for this yourself and me beguile?
For such an end did I erect this pile?
Did you so much despise me, in this fate
Myself with you not to associate?
Yourself and me, alas! this fatal wound,
The senate, and the people, doth confound.
I'll wash her wound with tears, and at her death,
My lips from hers shall draw her parting breath.'
Then with her vest the wound she wipes and dries;
Thrice with her arm the Queen attempts to rise,
But her strength failing, falls into a swound,
Life's last efforts yet striving with her wound;
Thrice on her bed she turns, with wand'ring sight
Seeking, she groans when she beholds the light.
Then Juno, pitying her disastrous fate,
Sends Iris down, her pangs to mitigate.
(Since if we fall before th'appointed day,
Nature and death continue long their fray.)
Iris descends; 'This fatal lock' (says she)
'To Pluto I bequeath, and set thee free;'
Then clips her hair: cold numbness strait bereaves
Her corpse of sense, and th'air her soul receives.

FOOTNOTE

[1] 'Cyllenius'—'God of thieves': Mercury.

[The following two pieces are translated from the Latin of Mancini, an Italian, contemporary with Petrarch.]

Wisdom's first progress is to take a view
What's decent or indecent, false or true.
He's truly prudent who can separate
Honest from vile, and still adhere to that;
Their difference to measure, and to reach
Reason well rectified must Nature teach.
And these high scrutinies are subjects fit
For man's all-searching and inquiring wit;
That search of knowledge did from Adam flow;
Who wants it yet abhors his wants to show.
Wisdom of what herself approves makes choice,
Nor is led captive by the common voice.
Clear-sighted Reason Wisdom's judgment leads,
And Sense, her vassal, in her footsteps treads.
That thou to Truth the perfect way may'st know,
To thee all her specific forms I'll show:
He that the way to honesty will learn,
First what's to be avoided must discern.
Thyself from flatt'ring self-conceit defend,
Nor what thou dost not know to know pretend.
Some secrets deep in abstruse darkness lie:
To search them thou wilt need a piercing eye.
Not rashly therefore to such things assent,
Which, undeceived, thou after may'st repent;
Study and time in these must thee instruct,
And others' old experience may conduct.
Wisdom herself her ear doth often lend
To counsel offer'd by a faithful friend.
In equal scales two doubtful matters lay,
Thou may'st choose safely that which most doth weigh;
'Tis not secure this place or that to guard,
If any other entrance stand unbarr'd:
He that escapes the serpent's teeth may fail,
If he himself secures not from his tail.
Who saith, who could such ill events expect?
With shame on his own counsels doth reflect.
Most in the world doth self-conceit deceive,
Who just and good whate'er they act believe;
To their wills wedded, to their errors slaves,
No man (like them) they think himself behaves.

This stiff-neck'd pride nor art nor force can bend,
Nor high-flown hopes to Reason's lure descend.
Fathers sometimes their children's faults regard
With pleasure, and their crimes with gifts reward.
Ill painters, when they draw, and poets write,
Virgil and Titian (self admiring) slight;
Then all they do like gold and pearl appears,
And others' actions are but dirt to theirs.
They that so highly think themselves above
All other men, themselves can only love;
Reason and virtue, all that man can boast
O'er other creatures, in those brutes are lost.
Observe (if thee this fatal error touch,
Thou to thyself contributing too much)
Those who are gen'rous, humble, just and wise,
Who not their gold, nor themselves idolise;
To form thyself by their example learn,
(For many eyes can more than one discern),
But yet beware of councils when too full,
Number makes long disputes, and graveness dull;
Though their advice be good, their counsel wise,
Yet length still loses opportunities:
Debate destroys despatch, as fruits we see
Rot when they hang too long upon the tree;
In vain that husbandman his seed doth sow,
If he his crop not in due season mow.
A gen'ral sets his army in array
In vain, unless he fight and win the day.
'Tis virtuous action that must praise bring forth,
Without which, slow advice is little worth.
Yet they who give good counsel praise deserve,
Though in the active part they cannot serve.
In action, learned counsellors their age,
Profession, or disease, forbids t'engage.
Nor to philosophers is praise denied,
Whose wise instructions after ages guide;
Yet vainly most their age in study spend;
No end of writing books, and to no end:
Beating their brains for strange and hidden things,
Whose knowledge, nor delight, nor profit brings;
Themselves with doubts both day and night perplex,
Nor gentle reader please, or teach, but vex.
Books should to one of these four ends conduce—
For wisdom, piety, delight, or use.
What need we gaze upon the spangled sky?
Or into matter's hidden causes pry?
To describe every city, stream, or hill
I' th'world, our fancy with vain arts to fill?

What is't to hear a sophister, that pleads,
Who by the ears the deceived audience leads?
If we were wise, these things we should not mind,
But more delight in easy matters find.
Learn to live well, that thou may'st die so too;
To live and die is all we have to do:
The way (if no digression's made) is even,
And free access, if we but ask, is given.
Then seek to know those things which make us bless'd,
And having found them, lock them in thy breast;
Inquiring then the way, go on, nor slack,
But mend thy pace, nor think of going back.
Some their whole age in these inquiries waste,
And die like fools before one step they've pass'd;
'Tis strange to know the way, and not t'advance;
That knowledge is far worse than ignorance.
The learned teach, but what they teach, not do,
And standing still themselves, make others go.
In vain on study time away we throw,
When we forbear to act the things we know.
The soldier that philosopher well blamed,
Who long and loudly in the schools declaim'd;
'Tell' (said the soldier) 'venerable Sir,
Why all these words, this clamour, and this stir?
Why do disputes in wrangling spend the day,
Whilst one says only yea, and t'other nay?'
'Oh,' said the doctor, 'we for wisdom toil'd,
For which none toils too much.' The soldier smiled;
'You're gray and old, and to some pious use
This mass of treasure you should now reduce:
But you your store have hoarded in some bank,
For which th'infernal spirits shall you thank.'
Let what thou learnest be by practice shown;
'Tis said that wisdom's children make her known.
What's good doth open to th'inquirer stand,
And itself offers to th'accepting hand;
All things by order and true measures done,
Wisdom will end, as well as she begun.
Let early care thy main concerns secure,
Things of less moment may delays endure:
Men do not for their servants first prepare,
And of their wives and children quit the care;
Yet when we're sick, the doctor's fetch'd in haste,
Leaving our great concernment to the last.
When we are well, our hearts are only set
(Which way we care not) to be rich, or great;
What shall become of all that we have got?
We only know that us it follows not;

And what a trifle is a moment's breath,
Laid in the scale with everlasting death!
What's time when on eternity we think!
A thousand ages in that sea must sink.
Time's nothing but a word; a million
Is full as far from infinite as one.
To whom thou much dost owe, thou much must pay,
Think on the debt against th'accounting day.
God, who to thee reason and knowledge lent,
Will ask how these two talents have been spent.
Let not low pleasures thy high reason blind,
He's mad, that seeks what no man e'er could find.
Why should we fondly please our sense, wherein
Beasts us exceed, nor feel the stings of sin?
What thoughts man's reason better can become,
Than th'expectation of his welcome home?
Lords of the world have but for life their lease,
And that too (if the lessor please) must cease.
Death cancels nature's bonds, but for our deeds
(That debt first paid) a strict account succeeds;
If here not clear'd, no suretyship can bail
Condemned debtors from th'eternal jail;
Christ's blood's our balsam; if that cure us here,
Him, when our judge, we shall not find severe;
His yoke is easy when by us embraced,
But loads and galls, if on our necks 'tis cast.
Be just in all thy actions, and if join'd
With those that are not, never change thy mind.
If ought obstruct thy course, yet stand not still,
But wind about, till you have topp'd the hill;
To the same end men sev'ral paths may tread,
As many doors into one temple lead;
And the same hand into a fist may close,
Which, instantly a palm expanded shows.
Justice and faith never forsake the wise,
Yet may occasion put him in disguise;
Not turning like the wind; but if the state
Of things must change, he is not obstinate;
Things past and future with the present weighs,
Nor credulous of what vain rumour says.
Few things by wisdom are at first believed;
An easy ear deceives, and is deceived:
For many truths have often pass'd for lies,
And lies as often put on truth's disguise;
As flattery too oft like friendship shows,
So them who speak plain truth we think our foes.
No quick reply to dubious questions make,
Suspense and caution still prevent mistake.

When any great design thou dost intend,
Think on the means, the manner, and the end:
All great concernments must delays endure;
Rashness and haste make all things unsecure;
And if uncertain thy pretensions be,
Stay till fit time wear out uncertainty;
But if to unjust things thou dost pretend,
Ere they begin let thy pretensions end.
Let thy discourse be such that thou may'st give
Profit to others, or from them receive:
Instruct the ignorant; to those that live
Under thy care, good rules and patterns give;
Nor is't the least of virtues, to relieve
Those whom afflictions or oppressions grieve.
Commend but sparingly whom thou dost love:
But less condemn whom thou dost not approve;
Thy friend, like flatt'ry, too much praise doth wrong,
And too sharp censure shows an evil tongue:
But let inviolate truth be always dear
To thee; e'en before friendship, truth prefer.
Than what thou mean'st to give, still promise less:
Hold fast thy power thy promise to increase.
Look forward what's to come, and back what's past,
Thy life will be with praise and prudence graced:
What loss or gain may follow, thou may'st guess,
Thou then wilt be secure of the success;
Yet be not always on affairs intent,
But let thy thoughts be easy, and unbent:
When our minds' eyes are disengaged and free,
They clearer, farther, and distinctly see;
They quicken sloth, perplexities untie,
Make roughness smooth, and hardness mollify;
And though our hands from labour are released,
Yet our minds find (even when we sleep) no rest.
Search not to find how other men offend,
But by that glass thy own offences mend;
Still seek to learn, yet care not much from whom,
(So it be learning) or from whence it come.
Of thy own actions, others' judgments learn;
Often by small, great matters we discern:
Youth what man's age is like to be doth show;
We may our ends by our beginnings know.
Let none direct thee what to do or say,
Till thee thy judgment of the matter sway;
Let not the pleasing many thee delight,
First judge if those whom thou dost please judge right.
Search not to find what lies too deeply hid,
Nor to know things whose knowledge is forbid;

Nor climb on pyramids, which thy head turn round
Standing, and whence no safe descent is found.
In vain his nerves and faculties he strains
To rise, whose raising unsecure remains:
They whom desert and favour forwards thrust,
Are wise, when they their measures can adjust.
When well at ease, and happy, live content,
And then consider why that life was lent.
When wealthy, show thy wisdom not to be
To wealth a servant, but make wealth serve thee.
Though all alone, yet nothing think or do,
Which nor a witness, nor a judge might know.
The highest hill is the most slipp'ry place,
And Fortune mocks us with a smiling face;
And her unsteady hand hath often placed
Men in high power, but seldom holds them fast;
Against her then her forces Prudence joins,
And to the golden mien herself confines.
More in prosperity is reason toss'd,
Than ships in storms, their helms and anchors lost:
Before fair gales not all our sails we bear,
But with side winds into safe harbours steer;
More ships in calms, on a deceitful coast,
Or unseen rocks, than in high storms are lost.
Who casts out threats and frowns no man deceives,
Time for resistance and defence he gives;
But flatt'ry still in sugar'd words betrays,
And poison in high-tasted meats conveys;
So Fortune's smiles unguarded man surprise,
But when she frowns, he arms, and her defies.

OF JUSTICE

'Tis the first sanction Nature gave to man,
Each other to assist in what they can;
Just or unjust, this law for ever stands;
All things are good by law which she commands;
The first step, man t'wards Christ must justly live,
Who t'us himself, and all we have, did give;
In vain doth man the name of just expect,
If his devotions he to God neglect;
So must we rev'rence God, as first to know
Justice from Him, not from ourselves, doth flow;
God those accepts who to mankind are friends,
Whose justice far as their own power extends;
In that they imitate the power Divine;

The sun alike on good and bad doth shine;
And he that doth no good, although no ill,
Does not the office of the just fulfil.
Virtue doth man to virtuous actions steer,
'Tis not enough that he should vice forbear;
We live not only for ourselves to care,
Whilst they that want it are denied their share.
Wise Plato said, the world with men was stored,
That succour each to other might afford;
Nor are those succours to one sort confined,
But sev'ral parts to sev'ral men consign'd;
He that of his own stores no part can give,
May with his counsel or his hands relieve.
If Fortune make thee powerful, give defence
'Gainst fraud and force, to naked innocence:
And when our Justice doth her tributes pay,
Method and order must direct the way.
First to our God we must with rev'rence bow;
The second honour to our prince we owe;
Next to wives, parents, children, fit respect,
And to our friends and kindred, we direct;
Then we must those who groan beneath the weight
Of age, disease, or want, commiserate.
'Mongst those whom honest lives can recommend,
Our Justice more compassion should extend;
To such, who thee in some distress did aid,
Thy debt of thanks with int'rest should be paid:
As Hesiod sings, spread waters o'er thy field,
And a most just and glad increase 'twill yield.
But yet take heed, lest doing good to one,
Mischief and wrong be to another done;
Such moderation with thy bounty join,
That thou may'st nothing give that is not thine;
That liberality's but cast away,
Which makes us borrow what we cannot pay.
And no access to wealth let rapine bring;
Do nothing that's unjust to be a king.
Justice must be from violence exempt,
But fraud's her only object of contempt.
Fraud in the fox, force in the lion dwells;
But Justice both from human hearts expels;
But he's the greatest monster (without doubt)
Who is a wolf within, a sheep without.
Nor only ill injurious actions are,
But evil words and slanders bear their share.
Truth Justice loves, and truth injustice fears,
Truth above all things a just man reveres.
Though not by oaths we God to witness call,

He sees and hears, and still remembers all;
And yet our attestations we may wrest
Sometimes to make the truth more manifest;
If by a lie a man preserve his faith,
He pardon, leave, and absolution hath;
Or if I break my promise, which to thee
Would bring no good, but prejudice to me.
All things committed to thy trust conceal,
Nor what's forbid by any means reveal.
Express thyself in plain, not doubtful words,
That ground for quarrels or disputes affords:
Unless thou find occasion, hold thy tongue;
Thyself or others careless talk may wrong.
When thou art called into public power,
And when a crowd of suitors throng thy door,
Be sure no great offenders 'scape their dooms;
Small praise from lenity and remissness comes;
Crimes pardon'd, others to those crimes invite,
Whilst lookers-on severe examples fright.
When by a pardon'd murd'rer blood is spilt,
The judge that pardon'd hath the greatest guilt;
Who accuse rigour, make a gross mistake;
One criminal pardon'd may an hundred make;
When justice on offenders is not done,
Law, government, and commerce, are o'erthrown;
As besieged traitors with the foe conspire,
T' unlock the gates, and set the town on fire.
Yet lest the punishment th'offence exceed,
Justice with weight and measure must proceed:
Yet when pronouncing sentence, seem not glad,
Such spectacles, though they are just, are sad;
Though what thou dost thou ought'st not to repent,
Yet human bowels cannot but relent:
Rather than all must suffer, some must die;
Yet Nature must condole their misery.
And yet, if many equal guilt involve,
Thou may'st not these condemn, and those absolve.
Justice, when equal scales she holds, is blind;
Nor cruelty, nor mercy, change her mind.
When some escape for that which others die,
Mercy to those, to these is cruelty.
A fine and slender net the spider weaves,
Which little and light animals receives;
And if she catch a common bee or fly,
They with a piteous groan and murmur die;
But if a wasp or hornet she entrap,
They tear her cords like Samson, and escape;
So like a fly the poor offender dies,

But like the wasp, the rich escapes and flies.
Do not, if one but lightly thee offend,
The punishment beyond the crime extend;
Or after warning the offence forget;
So God himself our failings doth remit.
Expect not more from servants than is just,
Reward them well, if they observe their trust;
Nor them with cruelty or pride invade,
Since God and Nature them our brothers made;
If his offence be great, let that suffice;
If light, forgive, for no man's always wise.

THE PROGRESS OF LEARNING

PREFACE

My early mistress, now my ancient Muse,
That strong Circæan liquor cease t'infuse,
Wherewith thou didst intoxicate my youth,
Now stoop with disenchanted wings to truth;
As the dove's flight did guide Aeneas, now
May thine conduct me to the golden bough:
Tell (like a tall old oak) how learning shoots
To heaven her branches, and to hell her roots.

When God from earth form'd Adam in the East,
He his own image on the clay impress'd;
As subjects then the whole creation came,
And from their natures Adam them did name,
Not from experience (for the world was new),
He only from their cause their natures knew.
Had memory been lost with innocence,
We had not known the sentence nor th'offence;
'Twas his chief punishment to keep in store
The sad remembrance what he was before;
And though th'offending part felt mortal pain,
Th' immortal part its knowledge did retain.
After the flood, arts to Chaldea fell;
The father of the faithful there did dwell,
Who both their parent and instructor was;
From thence did learning into Egypt pass:
Moses in all the Egyptian arts was skill'd,
When heavenly power that chosen vessel fill'd;
And we to his high inspiration owe,
That what was done before the flood we know.
Prom Egypt, arts their progress made to Greece,

Wrapp'd in the fable of the golden fleece.
Musæus first, then Orpheus, civilise
Mankind, and gave the world their deities;
To many gods they taught devotion,
Which were the distinct faculties of one;
Th' Eternal Cause, in their immortal lines
Was taught, and poets were the first divines:
God Moses first, then David, did inspire,
To compose anthems, for his heavenly choir;
To th'one the style of friend he did impart,
On th'other stamp the likeness of his heart:
And Moses, in the old original,
Even God the poet of the world doth call.
Next those old Greeks Pythagoras did rise,
Then Socrates, whom th'oracle call'd Wise;
The divine Plato moral virtue shows,
Then his disciple Aristotle rose,
Who Nature's secrets to the world did teach,
Yet that great soul our novelists impeach;
Too much manuring fill'd that field with weeds,
While sects, like locusts, did destroy the seeds;
The tree of knowledge, blasted by disputes,
Produces sapless leaves instead of fruits;
Proud Greece all nations else barbarians held,
Boasting her learning all the world excell'd.
Flying from thence[1] to Italy it came,
And to the realm of Naples gave the name,
Till both their nation and their arts did come
A welcome trophy to triumphant Rome;
Then whereso'er her conqu'ring eagles fled,
Arts, learning, and civility were spread;
And as in this our microcosm, the heart
Heat, spirit, motion gives to every part,
So Rome's victorious influence did disperse
All her own virtues through the universe.
Here some digression I must make, t'accuse
Thee, my forgetful, and ingrateful Muse:
Couldst thou from Greece to Latium take thy flight,
And not to thy great ancestor do right?
I can no more believe old Homer blind,
Than those who say the sun hath never shined;
The age wherein he lived was dark, but he
Could not want sight who taught the world to see:
They who Minerva from Jove's head derive,
Might make old Homer's skull the Muses' hive;
And from his brain that Helicon distil
Whose racy liquor did his offspring fill.
Nor old Anacreon, Hesiod, Theocrite,

Must we forget, nor Pindar's lofty flight.
Old Homer's soul, at last from Greece retired,
In Italy the Mantuan swain inspired.
When great Augustus made war's tempest cease,
His halcyon days brought forth the arts of peace;
He still in his triumphant chariot shines,
By Horace drawn, and Virgil's mighty lines.
'Twas certainly mysterious that the name [2]
Of prophets and of poets is the same;
What the tragedian[3]—wrote, the late success
Declares was inspiration, and not guess:
As dark a truth that author did unfold,
As oracles or prophets e'er foretold:
'At last the ocean shall unlock the bound
Of things, and a new world by Tiphys found,
Then ages far remote shall understand
The Isle of Thule is not the farthest land.'
Sure God, by these discov'ries, did design
That his clear light through all the world should shine,
But the obstruction from that discord springs
The prince of darkness made 'twixt Christian kings;
That peaceful age with happiness to crown,
From heaven the Prince of Peace himself came down,
Then the true sun of knowledge first appear'd,
And the old dark mysterious clouds were clear'd,
The heavy cause of th'old accursèd flood
Sunk in the sacred deluge of his blood.
His passion man from his first fall redeem'd;
Once more to paradise restored we seem'd;
Satan himself was bound, till th'iron chain
Our pride did break, and let him loose again.
Still the old sting remain'd, and man began
To tempt the serpent, as he tempted man;
Then Hell sends forth her furies, Av'rice, Pride,
Fraud, Discord, Force, Hypocrisy their guide;
Though the foundation on a rock were laid,
The church was undermined, and then betray'd:
Though the Apostles these events foretold,
Yet even the shepherd did devour the fold:
The fisher to convert the world began,
The pride convincing of vain-glorious man;
But soon his followers grew a sovereign lord,
And Peter's keys exchanged for Peter's sword,
Which still maintains for his adopted son
Vast patrimonies, though himself had none;
Wresting the text to the old giant's sense,
That heaven, once more, must suffer violence.
Then subtle doctors Scriptures made their prize;

Casuists, like cocks, struck out each others eyes;
Then dark distinctions reason's light disguised,
And into atoms truth anatomised.
Then Mah'met's crescent, by our feuds increased,
Blasted the learn'd remainders of the East;
That project, when from Greece to Rome it came,
Made Mother Ignorance Devotion's dame;
Then he whom Lucifer's own pride did swell,
His faithful emissary, rose from hell
To possess Peter's chair, that Hildebrand
Whose foot on mitres, then on crowns, did stand;
And before that exalted idol all
(Whom we call gods on earth) did prostrate fall.
Then darkness Europe's face did overspread
From lazy cells where superstition bred,
Which, link'd with blind obedience, so increased,
That the whole world some ages they oppress'd;
Till through these clouds the sun of knowledge brake,
And Europe from her lethargy did wake:
Then first our monarchs were acknowledged here,
That they their churches' nursing fathers were.
When Lucifer no longer could advance
His works on the false grounds of ignorance,
New arts he tries, and new designs he lays,
Then his well-studied masterpiece he plays;
Loyola, Luther, Calvin he inspires,
And kindles with infernal flames their fires,
Sends their forerunner (conscious of th'event)
Printing, his most pernicious instrument!
Wild controversy then, which long had slept,
Into the press from ruin'd cloisters leap'd;
No longer by implicit faith we err,
Whilst every man's his own interpreter;
No more conducted now by Aaron's rod,
Lay-elders from their ends create their god.
But seven wise men the ancient world did know,
We scarce know seven who think themselves not so.
When man learn'd undefiled religion,
We were commanded to be all as one;
Fiery disputes that union have calcined;
Almost as many minds as men we find,
And when that flame finds combustible earth,
Thence fatuus fires, and meteors take their birth;
Legions of sects and insects come in throngs;
To name them all would tire a hundred tongues.
So were the Centaurs of Ixion's race,
Who a bright cloud for Juno did embrace;
And such the monsters of Chimæra's kind,

Lions before, and dragons were behind.
Then from the clashes between popes and kings,
Debate, like sparks from flints' collision, springs:
As Jove's loud thunderbolts were forged by heat,
The like our Cyclops on their anvils beat;
All the rich mines of learning ransack'd are,
To furnish ammunition for this war:
Uncharitable zeal our reason whets,
And double edges on our passion sets;
'Tis the most certain sign the world's accursed,
That the best things corrupted are the worst;
'Twas the corrupted light of knowledge hurl'd
Sin, death, and ignorance o'er all the world;
That sun like this (from which our sight we have),
Gazed on too long, resumes the light he gave;
And when thick mists of doubts obscure his beams,
Our guide is error, and our visions, dreams;
'Twas no false heraldry when madness drew
Her pedigree from those who too much knew;
Who in deep mines for hidden knowledge toils,
Like guns o'ercharged, breaks, misses, or recoils;
When subtle wits have spun their thread too fine,
'Tis weak and fragile, like Arachne's line:
True piety, without cessation toss'd
By theories, the practic part is lost,
And like a ball bandied 'twixt pride and wit,
Rather than yield, both sides the prize will quit:
Then whilst his foe each gladiator foils,
The atheist looking on enjoys the spoils.
Through seas of knowledge we our course advance,
Discov'ring still new worlds of ignorance;
And these discov'ries make us all confess
That sublunary science is but guess;
Matters of fact to man are only known,
And what seems more is mere opinion;
The standers-by see clearly this event;
All parties say they're sure, yet all dissent;
With their new light our bold inspectors press,
Like Cham, to show their fathers' nakedness,
By whose example after ages may
Discover we more naked are than they;
All human wisdom to divine is folly;
This truth the wisest man made melancholy;
Hope, or belief, or guess, gives some relief,
But to be sure we are deceived brings grief:
Who thinks his wife is virtuous, though not so,
Is pleased and patient till the truth he know.
Our God, when heaven and earth he did create,

Form'd man who should of both participate;
If our lives' motions theirs must imitate,
Our knowledge, like our blood, must circulate.
When like a bridegroom from the east, the sun
Sets forth, he thither, whence he came, doth run;
Into earth's spongy veins the ocean sinks,
Those rivers to replenish which he drinks;
So learning, which from reason's fountain springs,
Back to the source some secret channel brings.
'Tis happy when our streams of knowledge flow
To fill their banks, but not to overthrow.

Ut metit Autumnus fruges quas parturit Aestas,
Sic ortum Natura, dedit Deus his quoque finem.

FOOTNOTES
[1]'From thence': Gracia Major.
[2] 'The name': Vates.
[3] 'The tragedian': Seneca.

ELEGY ON THE DEATH OF HENRY LORD HASTINGS, 1650

Reader, preserve thy peace: those busy eyes
Will weep at their own sad discoveries,
When every line they add improves thy loss,
Till, having view'd the whole, they seem a cross,
Such as derides thy passions' best relief,
And scorns the succours of thy easy grief;
Yet lest thy ignorance betray thy name
Of man and pious, read and mourn; the shame
Of an exemption from just sense doth show
Irrational, beyond excess of woe.
Since reason, then, can privilege a tear,
Manhood, uncensured, pay that tribute here
Upon this noble urn. Here, here remains
Dust far more precious than in India's veins;
Within those cold embraces, ravish'd, lies
That which completes the age's tyrannies;
Who weak to such another ill appear,
For what destroys our hope secures our fear.
What sin, unexpiated in this land
Of groans, hath guided so severe a hand?
The late great victim[1] that your altars knew,
Ye angry gods! might have excused this new
Oblation, and have spared one lofty light
Of virtue, to inform our steps aright;

By whose example good, condemnèd, we
Might have run on to kinder destiny.
But as the leader of the herd fell first
A sacrifice, to quench the raging thirst
Of inflamed vengeance for past crimes, so none
But this white, fatted youngling could atone,
By his untimely fate, that impious smoke,
That sullied earth, and did Heaven's pity choke.
Let it suffice for us that we have lost
In him more than the widow'd world can boast
In any lump of her remaining clay.
Fair as the gray-eyed morn he was; the day,
Youthful, and climbing upwards still, imparts
No haste like that of his increasing parts.
Like the meridian beam, his virtue's light
Was seen as full of comfort, and as bright.
Had his noon been as fixed, as clear—but he,
That only wanted immortality
To make him perfect, now submits to night,
In the black bosom of whose sable spite
He leaves a cloud of flesh behind, and flies,
Refined, all ray and glory, to the skies.
Great saint! shine there in an eternal sphere,
And tell those powers to whom thou now draw'st near,
That by our trembling sense, in Hastings dead,
Their anger and our ugly faults are read,
The short lines of whose life did to our eyes
Their love and majesty epitomise;
Tell them, whose stern decrees impose our laws;
The feasted grave may close her hollow jaws.
Though Sin search Nature, to provide her here
A second entertainment half so dear,
She'll never meet a plenty like this hearse,
Till Time present her with the universe!

FOOTNOTE
[1] 'Great victim': Charles I.

CATO, SCIPIO, LÆLIUS.

SCIPIO TO CATO.
Though all the actions of your life are crown'd
With wisdom, nothing makes them more renown'd,
Than that those years, which others think extreme,

Nor to yourself nor us uneasy seem;
Under which weight most, like th'old giants, groan.
When Aetna on their backs by Jove was thrown.

CATO
What you urge, Scipio, from right reason flows:
All parts of age seem burthensome to those
Who virtue's and true wisdom's happiness
Cannot discern; but they who those possess,
In what's impos'd by Nature find no grief,
Of which our age is (next our death) the chief,
Which though all equally desire t'obtain,
Yet when they have obtain'd it, they complain;
Such our inconstancies and follies are,
We say it steals upon us unaware:
Our want of reas'ning these false measures makes,
Youth runs to age, as childhood youth o'ertakes.
How much more grievous would our lives appear,
To reach th'eighth hundred, than the eightieth year?
Of what in that long space of time hath pass'd,
To foolish age will no remembrance last.
My age's conduct when you seem t'admire
(Which that it may deserve, I much desire),
'Tis my first rule, on Nature, as my guide
Appointed by the gods, I have relied;
And Nature (which all acts of life designs),
Not, like ill poets, in the last declines:
But some one part must be the last of all,
Which like ripe fruits, must either rot or fall.
And this from Nature must be gently borne,
Else her (as giants did the gods) we scorn.

LÆLIUS
But, Sir, 'tis Scipio's and my desire,
Since to long life we gladly would aspire,
That from your grave instructions we might hear,
How we, like you, may this great burthen bear.

CATO
This I resolved before, but now shall do
With great delight, since 'tis required by you.

LÆLIUS
If to yourself it will not tedious prove,
Nothing in us a greater joy can move,
That as old travellers the young instruct,
Your long, our short experience may conduct.

CATO

'Tis true (as the old proverb doth relate),
Equals with equals often congregate.
Two consuls[2] (who in years my equals were)
When senators, lamenting I did hear
That age from them had all their pleasures torn,
And them their former suppliants now scorn:
They what is not to be accused accuse,
Not others, but themselves their age abuse;
Else this might me concern, and all my friends,
Whose cheerful age with honour youth attends,
Joy'd that from pleasure's slav'ry they are free,
And all respects due to their age they see.
In its true colours, this complaint appears
The ill effect of manners, not of years;
For on their life no grievous burthen lies,
Who are well natured, temperate, and wise;
But an inhuman and ill-temper'd mind,
Not any easy part in life can find.

LÆLIUS

This I believe; yet others may dispute,
Their age (as yours) can never bear such fruit
Of honour, wealth, and power to make them sweet;
Not every one such happiness can meet.

CATO

Some weight your argument, my Lælius, bears,
But not so much as at first sight appears.
This answer by Themistocles was made,
(When a Seriphian thus did him upbraid,
'You those great honours to your country owe,
Not to yourself') 'Had I at Seripho[3]
Been born, such honour I had never seen,
Nor you, if an Athenian you had been;'
So age, clothed in indecent poverty,
To the most prudent cannot easy be;
But to a fool, the greater his estate,
The more uneasy is his age's weight.
Age's chief arts and arms are to grow wise,
Virtue to know, and known, to exercise;
All just returns to age then virtue makes,
Nor her in her extremity forsakes;
The sweetest cordial we receive at last,
Is conscience of our virtuous actions past.
I (when a youth) with reverence did look
On Quintus Fabius, who Tarentum took;
Yet in his age such cheerfulness was seen,

As if his years and mine had equal been;
His gravity was mix'd with gentleness,
Nor had his age made his good humour less;
Then was he well in years (the same that he
Was Consul that of my nativity),
(A stripling then), in his fourth consulate
On him at Capua I in arms did wait.
I five years after at Tarentum wan
The quæstorship, and then our love began;
And four years after, when I prætor was,
He pleaded, and the Cincian law[4] did pass.
With useful diligence he used t'engage,
Yet with the temperate arts of patient age
He breaks fierce Hannibal's insulting heats;
Of which exploit thus our friend Ennius treats:
He by delay restored the commonwealth,
Nor preferr'd rumour before public health.

FOOTNOTES
[1] This piece is adapted from Cicero, 'De Seucctute.'
[2] 'Two consuls': Caius Salinator, Spurius Albinus.
[3] 'Seripho': an isle to which condemned men were banished.
[4] 'Cincian law': against bribes.

THE ARGUMENT

When I reflect on age, I find there are
Four causes, which its misery declare.
I. Because our body's strength it much impairs:
II. That it takes off our minds from great affairs:
III. Next, that our sense of pleasure it deprives:
IV. Last, that approaching death attends our lives.

Of all these sev'ral causes I'll discourse,
And then of each, in order, weigh the force.

THE FIRST PART

The old from such affairs is only freed,
Which vig'rous youth and strength of body need;
But to more high affairs our age is lent,
Most properly when heats of youth are spent.
Did Fabius and your father Scipio
(Whose daughter my son married) nothing do?
Fabricii, Coruncani, Curii;
Whose courage, counsel, and authority,

The Roman commonwealth restored did boast,
Nor Appius, with whose strength his sight was lost,
Who when the Senate was to peace inclined
With Pyrrhus, shew'd his reason was not blind,
Whither's our courage and our wisdom come
When Rome itself conspires the fate of Rome?
The rest with ancient gravity and skill
He spake (for his oration's extant still).
'Tis seventeen years since he had Consul been
The second time, and there were ten between;
Therefore their argument's of little force,
Who age from great employments would divorce.
As in a ship some climb the shrouds, t'unfold
The sail, some sweep the deck, some pump the hold;
Whilst he that guides the helm employs his skill,
And gives the law to them by sitting still.
Great actions less from courage, strength, and speed,
Than from wise counsels and commands proceed;
Those arts age wants not, which to age belong,
Not heat but cold experience make us strong.
A Consul, Tribune, General, I have been,
All sorts of war I have pass'd through and seen;
And now grown old, I seem t'abandon it,
Yet to the Senate I prescribe what's fit.
I every day 'gainst Carthage war proclaim,
(For Rome's destruction hath been long her aim)
Nor shall I cease till I her ruin see,
Which triumph may the gods design for thee;
That Scipio may revenge his grandsire's ghost,
Whose life at Cannæ with great honour lost
Is on record; nor had he wearied been
With age, if he an hundred years had seen;
He had not used excursions, spears, or darts,
But counsel, order, and such aged arts,
Which, if our ancestors had not retain'd,
The Senate's name our council had not gain'd.
The Spartans to their highest magistrate
The name of Elder did appropriate:
Therefore his fame for ever shall remain,
How gallantly Tarentum he did gain,
With vig'lant conduct; when that sharp reply
He gave to Salinator, I stood by,
Who to the castle fled, the town being lost,
Yet he to Maximus did vainly boast,
'Twas by my means Tarentum you obtain'd;—
'Tis true, had you not lost, I had not gain'd.
And as much honour on his gown did wait,
As on his arms, in his fifth consulate.

When his colleague Carvilius stepp'd aside,
The Tribune of the people would divide
To them the Gallic and the Picene field;
Against the Senate's will he will not yield;
When, being angry, boldly he declares
Those things were acted under happy stars,
From which the commonwealth found good effects,
But otherwise they came from bad aspects.
Many great things of Fabius I could tell,
But his son's death did all the rest excel;
(His gallant son, though young, had Consul been)
His funeral oration I have seen
Often; and when on that I turn my eyes,
I all the old philosophers despise.
Though he in all the people's eyes seem'd great,
Yet greater he appear'd in his retreat;
When feasting with his private friends at home,
Such counsel, such discourse from him did come,
Such science in his art of augury,
No Roman ever was more learn'd than he;
Knowledge of all things present and to come,
Rememb'ring all the wars of ancient Rome,
Nor only there, but all the world's beside;
Dying in extreme age, I prophesied
That which is come to pass, and did discern
From his survivors I could nothing learn.
This long discourse was but to let you see
That his long life could not uneasy be.
Few like the Fabii or the Scipios are
Takers of cities, conquerors in war.
Yet others to like happy age arrive,
Who modest, quiet, and with virtue live:
Thus Plato writing his philosophy,
With honour after ninety years did die.
Th' Athenian story writ at ninety-four
By Isocrates, who yet lived five years more;
His master Gorgias at the hundredth year
And seventh, not his studies did forbear:
And, ask'd why he no sooner left the stage?
Said he saw nothing to accuse old age.
None but the foolish, who their lives abuse,
Age of their own mistakes and crimes accuse.
All commonwealths (as by records is seen)
As by age preserved, by youth destroy'd have been.
When the tragedian Nævius did demand,
Why did your commonwealth no longer stand?
'Twas answer'd, that their senators were new,
Foolish, and young, and such as nothing knew;

Nature to youth hot rashness doth dispense,
But with cold prudence age doth recompense.
But age, 'tis said, will memory decay,
So (if it be not exercised) it may;
Or, if by nature it be dull and slow.
Themistocles (when aged) the names did know
Of all th'Athenians; and none grow so old,
Not to remember where they hid their gold.
From age such art of memory we learn,
To forget nothing which is our concern;
Their interest no priest nor sorcerer
Forgets, nor lawyer, nor philosopher;
No understanding memory can want,
Where wisdom studious industry doth plant.
Nor does it only in the active live,
But in the quiet and contemplative;
When Sophocles (who plays when aged wrote)
Was by his sons before the judges brought,
Because he paid the Muses such respect,
His fortune, wife, and children to neglect;
Almost condemn'd, he moved the judges thus,
'Hear, but instead of me, my Oedipus.'
The judges hearing with applause, at th'end
Freed him, and said, 'No fool such lines had penn'd'.
What poets and what orators can I
Recount, what princes in philosophy,
Whose constant studies with their age did strive?
Nor did they those, though those did them survive.
Old husbandmen I at Sabinum know,
Who for another year dig, plough, and sow.
For never any man was yet so old,
But hoped his life one winter more might hold.
Cæcilius vainly said, 'Each day we spend
Discovers something, which must needs offend;'
But sometimes age may pleasant things behold,
And nothing that offends. He should have told
This not to age, but youth, who oft'ner see
What not alone offends, but hurts, than we.
That, I in him, which he in age condemn'd,
That us it renders odious, and contemn'd.
He knew not virtue, if he thought this truth;
For youth delights in age, and age in youth.
What to the old can greater pleasure be,
Than hopeful and ingenious youth to see,
When they with rev'rence follow where we lead,
And in straight paths by our directions tread?
And e'en my conversation here I see,
As well received by you, as yours by me.

'Tis disingenuous to accuse our age
Of idleness, who all our powers engage
In the same studies, the same course to hold;
Nor think our reason for new arts too old.
Solon the sage his progress never ceased,
But still his learning with his days increased;
And I with the same greediness did seek,
As water when I thirst, to swallow Greek;
Which I did only learn, that I might know
Those great examples which I follow now:
And I have heard that Socrates the wise,
Learn'd on the lute for his last exercise.
Though many of the ancients did the same,
To improve knowledge was my only aim.

THE SECOND PART

Now int' our second grievance I must break,
'That loss of strength makes understanding weak.'
I grieve no more my youthful strength to want,
Than, young, that of a bull, or elephant;
Then with that force content, which Nature gave,
Nor am I now displeased with what I have.
When the young wrestlers at their sport grew warm,
Old Milo wept, to see his naked arm;
And cried, 'twas dead. Trifler! thine heart and head,
And all that's in them (not thy arm) are dead;
This folly every looker on derides,
To glory only in thy arms and sides.
Our gallant ancestors let fall no tears,
Their strength decreasing by increasing years;
But they advanced in wisdom every hour,
And made the commonwealth advance in power.
But orators may grieve, for in their sides,
Rather than heads, their faculty abides;
Yet I have heard old voices loud and clear,
And still my own sometimes the Senate hear.
When th'old with smooth and gentle voices plead,
They by the ear their well-pleased audience lead:
Which, if I had not strength enough to do,
I could (my Lælius, and my Scipio)
What's to be done, or not be done, instruct,
And to the maxims of good life conduct.
Cneius and Publius Scipio, and (that man
Of men) your grandsire, the great African,
Were joyful when the flower of noble blood

Crowded their dwellings, and attending stood,
Like oracles their counsels to receive,
How in their progress they should act and live.
And they whose high examples youth obeys,
Are not despisèd, though their strength decays;
And those decays (to speak the naked truth,
Though the defects of age) were crimes of youth.
Intemp'rate youth (by sad experience found)
Ends in an age imperfect and unsound.
Cyrus, though aged (if Xenophon say true),
Lucius Metellus (whom when young I knew),
Who held (after his second consulate)
Twenty-two years the high pontificate;
Neither of these in body, or in mind,
Before their death the least decay did find.
I speak not of myself, though none deny
To age, to praise their youth the liberty:
Such an unwasted strength I cannot boast,
Yet now my years are eighty-four almost:
And though from what it was my strength is far,
Both in the first and second Punic war,
Nor at Thermopylæ, under Glabrio,
Nor when I Consul into Spain did go;
But yet I feel no weakness, nor hath length
Of winters quite enervated my strength;
And I, my guest, my client, or my friend,
Still in the courts of justice can defend:
Neither must I that proverb's truth allow,
'Who would be ancient, must be early so.'
I would be youthful still, and find no need
To appear old, till I was so indeed.
And yet you see my hours not idle are,
Though with your strength I cannot mine compare;
Yet this centurion's doth your's surmount,
Not therefore him the better man I count.
Milo when ent'ring the Olympic game,
With a huge ox upon his shoulder came.
Would you the force of Milo's body find,
Rather than of Pythagoras's mind?
The force which Nature gives with care retain,
But when decay'd, 'tis folly to complain.
In age to wish for youth is full as vain,
As for a youth to turn a child again.
Simple and certain Nature's ways appear,
As she sets forth the seasons of the year.
So in all parts of life we find her truth,
Weakness to childhood, rashness to our youth;
To elder years to be discreet and grave,

Then to old age maturity she gave.
(Scipio) you know, how Massinissa bears
His kingly port at more than ninety years;
When marching with his foot, he walks till night;
When with his horse, he never will alight;
Though cold or wet, his head is always bare;
So hot, so dry, his aged members are.
You see how exercise and temperance
Even to old years a youthful strength advance.
Our law (because from age our strength retires)
No duty which belongs to strength requires.
But age doth many men so feeble make,
That they no great design can undertake;
Yet that to age not singly is applied,
But to all man's infirmities beside.
That Scipio, who adopted you, did fall
Into such pains, he had no health at all;
Who else had equall'd Africanus' parts,
Exceeding him in all the lib'ral arts:
Why should those errors then imputed be
To age alone, from which our youth's not free?
Every disease of age we may prevent,
Like those of youth, by being diligent.
When sick, such mod'rate exercise we use,
And diet, as our vital heat renews;
And if our body thence refreshment finds,
Then must we also exercise our minds.
If with continual oil we not supply
Our lamp, the light for want of it will die;
Though bodies may be tired with exercise,
No weariness the mind could e'er surprise.
Cæcilius the comedian, when of age
He represents the follies on the stage,
They're credulous, forgetful, dissolute;
Neither those crimes to age he doth impute,
But to old men, to whom those crimes belong.
Lust, petulance, rashness, are in youth more strong
Than ago, and yet young men those vices hate,
Who virtuous are, discreet, and temperate:
And so, what we call dotage seldom breeds
In bodies, but where nature sow'd the seeds.
There are five daughters, and four gallant sons,
In whom the blood of noble Appius runs,
With a most num'rous family beside,
Whom he alone, though old and blind, did guide.
Yet his clear-sighted mind was still intent,
And to his business like a bow stood bent:
By children, servants, neighbours so esteem'd,

He not a master, but a monarch seem'd.
All his relations his admirers were,
His sons paid rev'rence, and his servants fear:
The order and the ancient discipline
Of Romans, did in all his actions shine.
Authority kept up old age secures,
Whose dignity as long as life endures.
Something of youth I in old age approve,
But more the marks of age in youth I love.
Who this observes may in his body find
Decrepit age, but never in his mind.
The seven volumes of my own reports,
Wherein are all the pleadings of our courts;
All noble monuments of Greece are come
Unto my hands, with those of ancient Rome.
The pontifical, and the civil law,
I study still, and thence orations draw;
And to confirm my memory, at night,
What I hear, see, or do, by day, recite.
These exercises for my thoughts I find;
These labours are the chariots of my mind.
To serve my friends, the Senate I frequent,
And there what I before digested vent;
Which only from my strength of mind proceeds,
Not any outward force of body needs;
Which, if I could not do, I should delight
On what I would to ruminate at night.
Who in such practices their minds engage,
Nor fear nor think of their approaching age,
Which by degrees invisibly doth creep:
Nor do we seem to die, but fall asleep.

THE THIRD PART

Now must I draw my forces 'gainst that host
Of pleasures, which i' th'sea of age are lost.
O thou most high transcendant gift of age!
Youth from its folly thus to disengage.
And now receive from me that most divine
Oration of that noble Tarentine,[1]
Which at Tarentum I long since did hear,
When I attended the great Fabius there.
Ye gods, was it man's nature, or his fate,
Betray'd him with sweet pleasure's poison'd bait?
Which he, with all designs of art or power,
Doth with unbridled appetite devour:

And as all poisons seek the noblest part,
Pleasure possesses first the head and heart;
Intoxicating both by them, she finds,
And burns the sacred temples of our minds.
Furies, which reason's divine chains had bound,
(That being broken) all the world confound.
Lust, murder, treason, avarice, and hell
Itself broke loose, in reason's palace dwell:
Truth, honour, justice, temperance, are fled,
All her attendants into darkness led.
But why all this discourse? when pleasure's rage
Hath conquer'd reason, we must treat with age.
Age undermines, and will in time surprise
Her strongest forts, and cut off all supplies;
And join'd in league with strong necessity,
Pleasure must fly, or else by famine die.
Flaminius, whom a consulship had graced,
(Then Censor) from the Senate I displaced;
When he in Gaul, a Consul, made a feast,
A beauteous courtesan did him request
To see the cutting off a pris'ner's head;
This crime I could not leave unpunished,
Since by a private villany he stain'd
That public honour which at Rome he gain'd.
Then to our age (when not to pleasures bent)
This seems an honour, not disparagement.
We not all pleasures like the Stoics hate,
But love and seek those which are moderate.
(Though divine Plato thus of pleasures thought,
They us, with hooks and baits, like fishes caught.)
When Questor, to the gods in public halls
I was the first who set up festivals.
Not with high tastes our appetites did force,
But fill'd with conversation and discourse;
Which feasts, Convivial Meetings we did name:
Not like the ancient Greeks, who to their shame,
Call'd it a Compotation, not a feast;
Declaring the worst part of it the best.
Those entertainments I did then frequent
Sometimes with youthful heat and merriment:
But now I thank my age, which gives me ease
From those excesses; yet myself I please
With cheerful talk to entertain my guests
(Discourses are to age continual feasts),
The love of meat and wine they recompense,
And cheer the mind, as much as those the sense.
I'm not more pleased with gravity among
The aged, than to be youthful with the young;

Nor 'gainst all pleasures proclaim open war,
To which, in age, some nat'ral motions are.
And still at my Sabinum I delight
To treat my neighbours till the depth of night.
But we the sense of gust and pleasure want,
Which youth at full possesses; this I grant;
But age seeks not the things which youth requires,
And no man needs that which he not desires.
When Sophocles was asked if he denied
Himself the use of pleasures, he replied,
'I humbly thank th'immortal gods, who me
From that fierce tyrant's insolence set free.'
But they whom pressing appetites constrain,
Grieve when they cannot their desires obtain.
Young men the use of pleasure understand,
As of an object new, and near at hand:
Though this stands more remote from age's sight,
Yet they behold it not without delight:
As ancient soldiers, from their duties eased,
With sense of honour and rewards are pleased;
So from ambitious hopes and lusts released,
Delighted with itself our age doth rest.
No part of life's more happy, when with bread
Of ancient knowledge and new learning fed;
All youthful pleasures by degrees must cease,
But those of age even with our years increase.
We love not loaded boards and goblets crown'd,
But free from surfeits our repose is sound.
When old Fabricius to the Samnites went
Ambassador, from Rome to Pyrrhus sent,
He heard a grave philosopher maintain,
That all the actions of our life were vain
Which with our sense of pleasure not conspired;
Fabricius the philosopher desired,
That he to Pyrrhus would that maxim teach,
And to the Samnites the same doctrine preach;
Then of their conquest he should doubt no more,
Whom their own pleasures overcame before.
Now into rustic matters I must fall,
Which pleasure seems to me the chief of all.
Age no impediment to those can give,
Who wisely by the rules of Nature live.
Earth (though our mother) cheerfully obeys
All the commands her race upon her lays.
For whatsoever from our hand she takes,
Greater or less, a vast return she makes.
Nor am I only pleased with that resource,
But with her ways, her method, and her force.

The seed her bosom (by the plough made fit)
Receives, where kindly she embraces it,
Which with her genuine warmth diffused and spread,
Sends forth betimes a green and tender head,
Then gives it motion, life, and nourishment,
Which from the root through nerves and veins are sent;
Straight in a hollow sheath upright it grows,
And, form receiving, doth itself disclose:
Drawn up in ranks and files, the bearded spikes
Guard it from birds as with a stand of pikes.
When of the vine I speak, I seem inspired,
And with delight, as with her juice, am fired;
At Nature's godlike power I stand amazed,
Which such vast bodies hath from atoms raised.
The kernel of a grape, the fig's small grain,
Can clothe a mountain and o'ershade a plain:
But thou, (dear Vine!) forbid'st me to be long;
Although thy trunk be neither large nor strong,
Nor can thy head (not help'd) itself sublime,
Yet, like a serpent, a tall tree can climb;
Whate'er thy many fingers can entwine,
Proves thy support, and all its strength is thine.
Though Nature gave not legs, it gave the hands,
By which thy prop the proudest cedar stands:
As thou hast hands, so hath thy offspring wings,
And to the highest part of mortals springs.
But lest thou should'st consume thy wealth in vain,
And starve thyself to feed a num'rous train,
Or like the bee (sweet as thy blood) design'd
To be destroy'd to propagate his kind,
Lest thy redundant and superfluous juice,
Should fading leaves instead of fruits produce,
The pruner's hand, with letting blood, must quench
Thy heat, and thy exub'rant parts retrench:
Then from the joints of thy prolific stem
A swelling knot is raisèd (call'd a gem),
Whence, in short space, itself the cluster shows,
And from earth's moisture mixed with sunbeams grows.
I' th'spring, like youth, it yields an acid taste,
But summer doth, like age, the sourness waste;
Then clothed with leaves, from heat and cold secure,
Like virgins, sweet and beauteous, when mature.
On fruits, flowers, herbs, and plants, I long could dwell,
At once to please my eye, my taste, my smell;
My walks of trees, all planted by my hand,
Like children of my own begetting stand.
To tell the sev'ral natures of each earth,
What fruits from each most properly take birth:

And with what arts to enrich every mould,
The dry to moisten, and to warm the cold.
But when we graft, or buds inoculate,
Nature by art we nobly meliorate;
As Orpheus' music wildest beasts did tame,
From the sour crab the sweetest apple came:
The mother to the daughter goes to school,
The species changed, doth her law overrule;
Nature herself doth from herself depart,
(Strange transmigration!) by the power of art.
How little things give law to great! we see
The small bud captivates the greatest tree.
Here even the power divine we imitate,
And seem not to beget, but to create.
Much was I pleased with fowls and beasts, the tame
For food and profit, and the wild for game.
Excuse me when this pleasant string I touch
(For age, of what delights it, speaks too much).
Who twice victorious Pyrrhus conquered,
The Sabines and the Samnites captive led,
Great Curius, his remaining days did spend,
And in this happy life his triumphs end.
My farm stands near, and when I there retire,
His, and that age's temper I admire:
The Samnites' chief, as by his fire he sate,
With a vast sum of gold on him did wait;
'Return,' said he, 'your gold I nothing weigh,
When those who can command it me obey.'
This my assertion proves, he may be old,
And yet not sordid, who refuses gold.
In summer to sit still, or walk, I love,
Near a cool fountain, or a shady grove.
What can in winter render more delight,
Than the high sun at noon, and fire at night?
While our old friends and neighbours feast and play,
And with their harmless mirth turn night to day,
Unpurchased plenty our full tables loads,
And part of what they lent, return t'our gods.
That honour and authority which dwells
With age, all pleasures of our youth excels.
Observe, that I that age have only praised
Whose pillars were on youth's foundations raised,
And that (for which I great applause received)
As a true maxim hath been since believed.
That most unhappy age great pity needs,
Which to defend itself, new matter pleads;
Not from gray hairs authority doth flow,
Nor from bald heads, nor from a wrinkled brow,

But our past life, when virtuously spent,
Must to our age those happy fruits present.
Those things to age most honourable are,
Which easy, common, and but light appear,
Salutes, consulting, compliment, resort,
Crowding attendance to and from the court:
And not on Rome alone this honour waits,
But on all civil and well-govern'd states.
Lysander, pleading in his city's praise,
From thence his strongest argument did raise,
That Sparta did with honour age support,
Paying them just respect at stage and court.
But at proud Athens youth did age outface,
Nor at the plays would rise, or give them place.
When an Athenian stranger of great age
Arrived at Sparta, climbing up the stage,
To him the whole assembly rose, and ran
To place and ease this old and rev'rend man,
Who thus his thanks returns, 'Th' Athenians know
What's to be done, but what they know not do.'
Here our great Senate's orders I may quote,
The first in age is still the first in vote.
Nor honour, nor high birth, nor great command,
In competition with great years may stand.
Why should our youth's short, transient, pleasures dare
With age's lasting honours to compare?
On the world's stage, when our applause grows high,
For acting here life's tragic-comedy,
The lookers-on will say we act not well,
Unless the last the former scenes excel:
But age is froward, uneasy, scrutinous,
Hard to be pleased, and parsimonious;
But all those errors from our manners rise,
Not from our years; yet some morosities
We must expect, since jealousy belongs
To age, of scorn, and tender sense of wrongs:
Yet these are mollified, or not discern'd,
Where civil arts and manners have been learn'd:
So the Twins' humours,[2] in our Terence, are
Unlike-this harsh and rude, that smooth and fair.
Our nature here is not unlike our wine,
Some sorts, when old, continue brisk and fine;
So age's gravity may seem severe,
But nothing harsh or bitter ought t'appear.
Of age's avarice I cannot see
What colour, ground, or reason there should be:
Is it not folly, when the way we ride
Is short, for a long voyage to provide?

To avarice some title youth may own,
To reap in autumn what the spring had sown;
And, with the providence of bees, or ants,
Prevent with summer's plenty winter's wants.
But age scarce sows till death stands by to reap,
And to a stranger's hand transfers the heap;
Afraid to be so once, she's always poor,
And to avoid a mischief makes it sure.
Such madness, as for fear of death to die,
Is to be poor for fear of poverty.

FOOTNOTES

[1] 'Tarentine': Archytas, much praised by Horace.
[2] 'Twins' humours': in his comedy called 'Adelphi.'

THE FOURTH PART

Now against (that which terrifies our age)
The last, and greatest grievance, we engage;
To her grim Death appears in all her shapes,
The hungry grave for her due tribute gapes.
Fond, foolish man! with fear of death surprised,
Which either should be wish'd for, or despised;
This, if our souls with bodies death destroy;
That, if our souls a second life enjoy.
What else is to be fear'd, when we shall gain
Eternal life, or have no sense of pain?
The youngest in the morning are not sure
That till the night their life they can secure;
Their age stands more exposed to accidents
Than ours, nor common care their fate prevents:
Death's force (with terror) against Nature strives,
Nor one of many to ripe age arrives.
From this ill fate the world's disorders rise,
For if all men were old, they would be wise;
Years and experience our forefathers taught,
Them under laws and into cities brought:
Why only should the fear of death belong
To age, which is as common to the young?
Your hopeful brothers, and my son, to you
(Scipio) and me, this maxim makes too true:
But vig'rous youth may his gay thoughts erect
To many years, which age must not expect.
But when he sees his airy hopes deceived,
With grief he says, Who this would have believed?
We happier are than they, who but desired

To possess that which we long since acquired.
What if our age to Nestor's could extend?
'Tis vain to think that lasting which must end;
And when 'tis past, not any part remains
Thereof, but the reward which virtue gains.
Days, months, and years, like running waters flow,
Nor what is past, nor what's to come, we know:
Our date, how short soe'er, must us content.
When a good actor doth his part present,
In every act he our attention draws,
That at the last he may find just applause;
So (though but short) yet we must learn the art
Of virtue, on the stage to act our part;
True wisdom must our actions so direct,
Not only the last plaudit to expect;
Yet grieve no more, though long that part should last,
Than husbandmen, because the spring is past.
The spring, like youth, fresh blossoms doth produce,
But autumn makes them ripe and fit for use:
So age a mature mellowness doth set
On the green promises of youthful heat.
All things which Nature did ordain, are good,
And so must be received and understood.
Age, like ripe apples, on earth's bosom drops,
While force our youth, like fruits untimely, crops;
The sparkling flame of our warm blood expires,
As when huge streams are pour'd on raging fires;
But age unforced falls by her own consent,
As coals to ashes, when the spirit's spent;
Therefore to death I with such joy resort,
As seamen from a tempest to their port.
Yet to that port ourselves we must not force,
Before our pilot, Nature, steers our course.
Let us the causes of our fear condemn,
Then Death at his approach we shall contemn.
Though to our heat of youth our age seems cold,
Yet when resolved, it is more brave and bold.
Thus Solon to Pisistratus replied,
Demanded, on what succour he relied,
When with so few he boldly did engage?
He said, he took his courage from his age.
Then death seems welcome, and our nature kind,
When, leaving us a perfect sense and mind,
She (like a workman in his science skill'd)
Pulls down with ease what her own hand did build.
That art which knew to join all parts in one,
Makes the least vi'lent separation.
Yet though our ligaments betimes grow weak,

We must not force them till themselves they break.
Pythagoras bids us in our station stand,
Till God, our general, shall us disband.
Wise Solon dying, wish'd his friends might grieve,
That in their memories he still might live.
Yet wiser Ennius gave command to all
His friends not to bewail his funeral;
Your tears for such a death in vain you spend,
Which straight in immortality shall end.
In death, if there be any sense of pain,
But a short space to age it will remain;
On which, without my fears, my wishes wait,
But tim'rous youth on this should meditate:
Who for light pleasure this advice rejects,
Finds little, when his thoughts he recollects.
Our death (though not its certain date) we know;
Nor whether it may be this night, or no:
How then can they contented live, who fear
A danger certain, and none knows how near?
They err, who for the fear of death dispute,
Our gallant actions this mistake confute.
Thee, Brutus! Rome's first martyr I must name;
The Curtii bravely dived the gulf of flame:
Attilius sacrificed himself, to save
That faith, which to his barb'rous foes he gave;
With the two Scipios did thy uncle fall,
Rather than fly from conqu'ring Hannibal.
The great Marcellus (who restorèd Rome)
His greatest foes with honour did entomb.
Their lives how many of our legions threw
Into the breach, whence no return they knew?
Must then the wise, the old, the learned fear,
What not the rude, the young, th'unlearn'd forbear?
Satiety from all things else doth come,
Then life must to itself grow wearisome.
Those trifles wherein children take delight,
Grow nauseous to the young man's appetite;
And from those gaieties our youth requires
To exercise their minds, our age retires.
And when the last delights of age shall die,
Life in itself will find satiety.
Now you (my friends) my sense of death shall hear,
Which I can well describe, for he stands near.
Your father, Lælius, and your's, Scipio,
My friends, and men of honour, I did know;
As certainly as we must die, they live
That life which justly may that name receive:
Till from these prisons of our flesh released,

Our souls with heavy burdens lie oppress'd;
Which part of man from heaven falling down,
Earth, in her low abyss, doth hide and drown,
A place so dark to the celestial light,
And pure, eternal fire's quite opposite,
The gods through human bodies did disperse
An heavenly soul, to guide this universe,
That man, when he of heavenly bodies saw
The order, might from thence a pattern draw:
Nor this to me did my own dictates show,
But to the old philosophers I owe.
I heard Pythagoras, and those who came
With him, and from our country took their name;
Who never doubted but the beams divine,
Derived from gods, in mortal breasts did shine.
Nor from my knowledge did the ancients hide
What Socrates declared the hour he died;
He th'immortality of souls proclaim'd,
(Whom th'oracle of men the wisest named)
Why should we doubt of that whereof our sense
Finds demonstration from experience?
Our minds are here, and there, below, above;
Nothing that's mortal can so swiftly move.
Our thoughts to future things their flight direct,
And in an instant all that's past collect.
Reason, remembrance, wit, inventive art,
No nature, but immortal, can impart.
Man's soul in a perpetual motion flows,
And to no outward cause that motion owes;
And therefore that no end can overtake,
Because our minds cannot themselves forsake.
And since the matter of our soul is pure
And simple, which no mixture can endure
Of parts, which not among themselves agree;
Therefore it never can divided be.
And Nature shows (without philosophy)
What cannot be divided, cannot die.
We even in early infancy discern
Knowledge is born with babes before they learn;
Ere they can speak they find so many ways
To serve their turn, and see more arts than days:
Before their thoughts they plainly can express,
The words and things they know are numberless;
Which Nature only and no art could find,
But what she taught before, she call'd to mind,
These to his sons (as Xenophon records)
Of the great Cyrus were the dying words;
'Fear not when I depart (nor therefore mourn)

I shall be nowhere, or to nothing turn:
That soul which gave me life, was seen by none,
Yet by the actions it design'd was known;
And though its flight no mortal eye shall see,
Yet know, for ever it the same shall be.
That soul which can immortal glory give
To her own virtues must for ever live.
Can you believe that man's all-knowing mind
Can to a mortal body be confined?
Though a foul foolish prison her immure
On earth, she (when escaped) is wise and pure.
Man's body when dissolved is but the same
With beasts, and must return from whence it came;
But whence into our bodies reason flows,
None sees it when it comes, or where it goes.
Nothing resembles death so much as sleep,
Yet then our minds themselves from slumber keep.
When from their fleshly bondage they are free,
Then what divine and future things they see!
Which makes it most apparent whence they are,
And what they shall hereafter be, declare.'
This noble speech the dying Cyrus made.
Me (Scipio) shall no argument persuade,
Thy grandsire, and his brother, to whom Fame
Gave, from two conquer'd parts o' th'world, their name,
Nor thy great grandsire, nor thy father Paul,
Who fell at Cannæ against Hannibal;
Nor I (for 'tis permitted to the aged
To boast their actions) had so oft engaged
In battles, and in pleadings, had we thought,
That only fame our virtuous actions bought;
'Twere better in soft pleasure and repose
Ingloriously our peaceful eyes to close:
Some high assurance hath possess'd my mind,
After my death an happier life to find.
Unless our souls from the immortals came,
What end have we to seek immortal fame?
All virtuous spirits some such hope attends,
Therefore the wise his days with pleasure ends.
The foolish and short-sighted die with fear,
That they go nowhere, or they know not where.
The wise and virtuous soul, with clearer eyes,
Before she parts, some happy port descries.
My friends, your fathers I shall surely see:
Nor only those I loved, or who loved me,
But such as before ours did end their days,
Of whom we hear, and read, and write their praise.
This I believe; for were I on my way,

None should persuade me to return, or stay:
Should some god tell me that I should be born
And cry again, his offer I would scorn;
Asham'd, when I have ended well my race,
To be led back to my first starting-place.
And since with life we are more grieved than joy'd,
We should be either satisfied or cloy'd:
Yet will I not my length of days deplore,
As many wise and learn'd have done before:
Nor can I think such life in vain is lent,
Which for our country and our friends is spent.
Hence from an inn, not from my home, I pass,
Since Nature meant us here no dwelling-place.
Happy when I, from this turmoil set free,
That peaceful and divine assembly see:
Not only those I named I there shall greet,
But my own gallant virtuous Cato meet.
Nor did I weep, when I to ashes turn'd
His belov'd body, who should mine have burn'd.
I in my thoughts beheld his soul ascend,
Where his fixed hopes our interview attend:
Then cease to wonder that I feel no grief
From age, which is of my delights the chief.
My hopes if this assurance hath deceived
(That I man's soul immortal have believed),
And if I err, no power shall dispossess
My thoughts of that expected happiness,
Though some minute philosophers pretend,
That with our days our pains and pleasures end.
If it be so, I hold the safer side,
For none of them my error shall deride.
And if hereafter no rewards appear,
Yet virtue hath itself rewarded here.
If those who this opinion have despised,
And their whole life to pleasure sacrificed,
Should feel their error, they, when undeceived,
Too late will wish that me they had believed.
If souls no immortality obtain,
'Tis fit our bodies should be out of pain.
The same uneasiness which everything
Gives to our nature, life must also bring.
Good acts, if long, seem tedious; so is age,
Acting too long upon this earth her stage.—
Thus much for age, to which when you arrive,
That joy to you, which it gives me, 'twill give.

Next to those poets who have exerted an influence on the matter, should be ranked those who have improved the manner, of our song. So that thus the same list may include the names of a Chaucer and a Waller, of a Milton and a Denham—the more as we suspect none but a true poet can materially improve even a poetical mode, can contrive even a new stirrup to Pegasus, or even to retune the awful organ of Pythia. Neither Denham nor Waller were great poets; but they have produced lines and verses so good, and have, besides, exerted an influence so considerable on modern versification, and the style of poetical utterance, that they are entitled to a highly respectable place amidst the sons of British song.

Sir John Denham, although thoroughly English both in descent and in complexion of mind, was born in Dublin in 1615. His father, whose name also was Sir John (of Little Horseley, in Essex), was, at the time of our poet's birth, the Chief Baron of Exchequer in Ireland. His mother was Eleanor More, daughter of Sir Garret More, Baron of Mellefont. Two years after the son's birth, the father, being made an English Baron of Exchequer, returned to his native country, and educated young John in London. Thence, at the age of sixteen, he went to study at Oxford, where he became celebrated rather for dissipation than diligence. He was, although a youth of imaginative temperament, excessively fond of gambling; and it was said of him, that he was more given to "dreams and dice than to study." His future eminence might be foreseen by some of his friends; but, in general, men looked on him rather as an idle and misled youth of fortune, than as a genius. Three years after, he removed to Lincoln's Inn, where he continued occasionally to gamble, and was sometimes punished for his pains, being plundered by more skilful or unscrupulous gamesters, but did not forget his studies. His conscience, on one occasion, aroused by a rebuke from a friend, awoke; and, to confirm the resolutions which it forced upon him, he wrote and published an "Essay on Gaming." In this respect he resembles Sir Richard Steele when a young soldier, who, in order to cure himself of his dissipations, wrote and published "The Christian Hero"—his object being, by drawing the picture of a character exactly opposite to his own, to commit himself irrevocably to virtue, and to break down all the bridges between him and a return to vice. It is, alas! notorious, that Steele's holiness turned out only to be a FIT, of not much longer duration than a morning headache, and that the "Christian Hero" remains not as a model to which its author's conduct was ever conformed, but as a severe, self-written satire on his whole career. And so with Denham. For some time he forsook the gambling-table, and applied his attention partly to law, and partly to poetry, translating, in 1636, the "Second Book of the Aeneid;" but when his father died, two years afterwards, and left him some thousands, he rushed again to the dice-box, and melted them as rapidly as the wind melts the snow of spring.

"In 1642 he broke out," as Waller remarks of him, "like the Irish Rebellion, threescore thousand strong, when nobody was aware, or in the least suspected it," in the play of "Sophy;" and, sooth to say, like that rebellion, his outbreak is lawless and irregular, as well as strong; as in that rebellion, too, there is a rather needless expenditure of blood. What Byron says of Dr. Polidori's tragedy, is nearly true of "Sophy"—

"All stab, and everybody dies."

Nothing can be more horrible and disgusting than many of the incidents. A father suspecting and plotting against a dear and noble son; a son deprived of sight by the command of a father, and meditating in his rage and revenge the murder of his own favourite daughter, because she is beloved by his father; and the deaths of both son and father by poison, administered through means of a courtier who has betrayed both. Such are the main hinges on which the plot of the piece turns. The versification, too, is exceedingly unequal; sometimes swelling into rather full and splendid blank verse, and anon shrinking up into lines stunted and shrivelled, like boughs either touched by frost, or lopped by the axe of the woodman. Still there are in "Sophy" a force of style, a maturity of mind, an energy of declamation, and, here and there, an appreciation of Shakspeare—shewn in a generous though hopeless rivalry of his manner— which account for the reception it at first met with, and seem to have excited in Denham's contemporaries expectations which were never fulfilled. This uprise, as well as that of the Irish (which took place the year before it), turned out, on the whole, abortive. And yet what fine lines and sentiments are the following, culled from "Sophy" almost ad aperturam libri:—

"Fear and guilt
Are the same thing, and when our actions are not,
Our fears are crimes.
The east and west
Upon the globe, a mathematic point
Only divides; thus happiness and misery,
And all extremes, are still contiguous.

More gallant actions have been lost, for want of being
Completely wicked, than have been performed
By being exactly virtuous. 'Tis hard to be
Exact in good, or excellent in ill;
Our will wants power, or else our power wants skill.

When in the midst of fears we are surprised
With unexpected happiness, the first
Degrees of joy are mere astonishment.
Fear, the shadow
Of danger, like the shadow of our bodies,
Is greater, then, when that which is the cause
Is farthest off."

The blinded prince's soliloquy, in the first scene of the fifth act, is worthy of Shakspeare. We must quote the following lines:—

"Reason, my soul's eye, still sees
Clearly, and clearer for the want of eyes,
For gazing through the windows of the body
It met such several, such distracting objects;
But now confined within itself it sees
A strange and unknown world, and there discovers
Torrents of anger, mountains of ambition,
Gulfs of desire, and towers of hope, large giants,
Monsters and savage beasts; to vanquish these
Will be a braver conquest, than the old
Or the new world."

Shortly after the appearance of "Sophy," he was admitted, by the form then usual, Sheriff of Surrey, and appointed governor of Farnham Castle for the king; this important post, however, he soon resigned, and retreated to Oxford, where, in 1643, he published his poem entitled "Cooper's Hill." This instantly became popular, and many who might have seen in "Sophy" greater powers than were disclosed in this new effort, envied its fame, and gave out that he had bought it of a vicar for forty pounds. For this there was, of course, no proof, and it is only worth mentioning because it is one of a large class of cases, in which envious mediocrity, or crushed dulness, or jealous rivalry, has sought to snatch hard-won laurels from the brow of genius. As if these laurels were so smooth, and so soothing, as always to invite ambition, or as if they were so flexible as to suit every brow! As if FIRE lurked not sometimes in their leaves, and as if there were not, besides, a nobler jealousy in the public mind ready to watch and to avenge their misappropriation. Certain it is that not only, as Johnson remarks, was the attempt made to rob Addison of "Cato," and Pope of the "Essay of Criticism," but it has a hundred times taken place in the history of poetry. Rolt, as we saw in our late life of Akenside, tried to snatch the honour of writing "The Pleasures of Imagination" from its author. Lauder accused Milton of plundering the Italians wholesale. Scott's early novels have only the other day been most absurdly claimed for his brother Thomas. And notwithstanding Shakspeare's well-known lines over his sepulchre at Stratford—

"Bless'd be the man who spares these stones,
But curs'd be he who moves my bones"—

a worse outrage has been recently committed on his memory, than were his dust, like Wickliffe's, tossed out of his tomb into the Avon—his plays have been, with as much stupidity as malice, attributed to Lord Bacon! Homer, too, has been found out to be a myth; and we know not if even Dante's originality has altogether passed unquestioned in this age of disbelief and downpulling; although what brow, save that thunder-scathed pile, could wear those scorched laurels, and who but the "man who had been in hell" could have written the "Inferno?" Worst of all, a class of writers have of late sought to prove that there is no such thing as originality—that genius means just dexterous borrowing-that the "Appropriation Clause" is of divine right—and have certainly proved themselves true to their own principles.

In 1647, circumstances brought our poet more closely in connexion with the royal family, and on one occasion he carried a message from the Queen to King Charles, then in prison. He subsequently conducted, with great success, the King's correspondence; and in April 1648 he conveyed the young Duke of York (afterwards James II.) from London to France, and delivered him to the charge of the Queen and the Prince of Wales. He had, ere leaving Britain, written a translation of Cato-Major on Old Age. While in France, attending on the exiled prince, he wrote a number of poetical pieces at his master's desire; among others, a song in honour of an embassy to Poland, which he and Lord Crofts undertook for Charles II., and during which they are said to have collected £10,000 for the royal cause from the Scotchmen who then abounded in that country as travelling merchants or pedlars. Meanwhile his political misdemeanours were punished by the Parliament confiscating the remnant of his estate. In 1652, he returned to England penniless, and was supported by the Earl of Pembroke. After the Restoration, Charles, more mindful of him than of many of his friends and the partners of his exile, bestowed on Denham the Surveyorship of the King's Buildings and the Order of the Bath. The situation of Surveyor, even in his careless and improvident hands, turned out a lucrative one; for it is said that he cleared by it no less than £7000. Of his first wife, we hear little or nothing; but about this time, flushed as he was with prosperity, and the popularity of the writings he continued to produce, he contracted a second marriage, which was so far from happy that its consequences led to a fit of temporary derangement. Butler, then a disappointed and exacerbated man, was malignant enough to lampoon him for lunacy—an act which, Dr. Johnson well remarks, "no provocation could excuse." It was, in Fuller's fine old quaint language, "breaking one whom God had bowed before." Our readers will find Butler's squib in our edition of that poet, vol. ii. p. 200, under the title of "A Panegyrick on Sir John Denham's

Recovery from his Madness." It is a piece quite unworthy of Butler's powers, and its sting lies principally in charging Denham with plagiarising "Cooper's Hill" and "Sophy," with gambling, and with overreaching the King as Surveyor of the Public Buildings, and with an overbearing and quarrelsome temper—but it contains no allusion to his domestic infelicity. Some have hinted that the cause of his insanity lay in jealousy—that Denham suspected his wife to be too intimate with the Duke of York—that he poisoned her, and maddened in remorse. Whatever the cause, the distemper was not of long continuance. He recovered in time to write some verses on the death of Cowley, which took place in 1667; but in the next year he himself expired, and was buried by the side of his friend in Westminster Abbey, not very far from Chaucer and Spencer. His funeral took place on the 19th of March 1668. He had attained the age of fifty-three.

This is all we can definitely state of the history of Sir John Denham, and certainly the light it casts on his character is neither very plentiful nor very pleasing. A gambler in his early days, he became a political intriguer, an unhappy husband, a maniac, and died in the prime of life. It need only further be recorded of him, that, according to some accounts, he first discovered the merits of Milton's "Paradise Lost," and went about with the book new from the press in his hands, shewing it to everybody, and exclaiming, "This beats us all, and the ancients too!" If this story be true, it says as much for his heart as his head for the generous disposition which made him praise a political adversary, as for the critical taste which discerned at a glance the value of the world's greatest poem. On the whole, however, Denham as a man stands on the same general level with the Cavalier wits in the days of Charles. If he did not rise so high as Cowley, he did not sink so low as Rochester, or even as Butler.

We may now regret, both that he did not live better, and that he did not write more. He had unquestionably in him greater powers than he ever expressed in his works. These are few, fragmentary, and unequal; but, nevertheless, must be reckoned productions of no ordinary merit. They discover a great deal of the body, and not a little of the soul, of poetry. In the passages we cited from "Sophy," and throughout the whole of that play, there is a vigorous and profound vein of reflection, as well as of imagination. Like Shakspeare, although on a scale very much inferior, he carries on a constant stream of subtle reflection amidst all the windings of his story; and even the most critical points of the drama are studded with pearls. Coleridge speaks of himself, or some one else, as wishing to live "collaterally, or aside, to the onward progress of society;" and thus, in the drama, there should ever be, as it were, a projection, or alias, of the author standing collaterally, or aside, to the bustling incidents and whirling passions, and calmly adding the commentary of wisdom, as they rush impetuously on. Such essentially was the chorus of the ancient Greek play; and a similar end is answered in Shakspeare by the subtle asides, the glancing bye-lights, which his wondrous intellect interposes amidst the rapid play of his fancy, the exuberance of his wit, and the crowded incident and interchange of passion created by his genius. Some have maintained that the philosophy of a drama should be chiefly confined to the conceptions of the characters, the development of the plot, and the management of the dialogue—that all the reflection should be molten into the mass of the play, and none of it embossed on the surface; but certainly neither Shakspeare's, nor Schiller's, nor Goethe's dramas answer to this ideal—all of them, besides the philosophy, so to speak, afoot in the progress of the story, contain a great deal standing still, quietly lurking in nooks and corners, and yet exerting a powerful influence on the ultimate effect and explanation of the whole. And so, according to its own proportions, it is with Denham's "Sophy." Indeed, as we have above hinted, its power lies more in these interesting individual beauties than in its general structure.

"Cooper's Hill," next to "Sophy," is undoubtedly his best production. Dr. Johnson calls it the first English specimen of local poetry—i.e., of poetry in which a special scene is, through the embellishments of traditionary recollection, moral reflections, and the power of association generally, uplifted into a poetical light. This has been done afterwards by Garth, in his "Claremont;" Pope, in his "Windsor Forest;" Dyer, in his "Gronger-hill," and a hundred other instances. The great danger in this class of poems, is lest imported sentiment and historical reminiscence should overpower the living lineaments, and all but blot out the memory of the actual landscape. And so it is to some extent in "Cooper's Hill," the scene beheld from which is speedily lost in a torrent of political reflection and moralising. The well-known lines on the Thames are rhetorical and forcible, but not, we think, highly poetical:—

"Oh, could I flow like thee, and make thy stream
My great example, as it is my theme!
Though deep, yet clear, though gentle, yct not dull,
Strong without rage, without o'erflowing full."

The poem closes with another river-picture, which some will admire:—

"When a calm river, raised with sudden rains
Or snows dissolved, o'erflows the adjoining plains,
The husbandmen, with high-raised banks, secure
Their greedy hopes, and this he can endure;
But, if with bays and dams they strive to force
His channel to a new or narrow course,
No longer then—within his banks he dwells,
First to a torrent, then a deluge swells,
Stronger and fiercer by restraint he roars,
And knows no bound, but makes his power his shores."

Again, he says of Thames:—

"Thames, the most loved of all the ocean's sons
By his old sire, to his embraces runs,
Hasting to pay his tribute to the sea,
Like mortal life to meet eternity.
Though with those streams he no resemblance hold
Whose foam is amber and their gravel gold.
His genuine and less guilty wealth t'explore,
Search not his bottom, but survey his shore."

Yet, though fond of, and great in, describing rivers, he is not, after all, the "river-god" of poetry. Professor Wilson speaks with a far deeper voice:—

"Down falls the drawbridge with a thund'ring shock,
And, in an instant, ere the eye can know,
Binds the stern castle to the opposing rock,
And hangs in calmness o'er the flood below;
A raging flood, that, born among the hills,
Flows dancing on through many a nameless glen,
Till, join'd by all his tributary rills
From lake and tarn, from marsh and from fen,

He leaves his empire with a kingly glee,
And fiercely bids retire the billows of the sea!"

Different poets are made to write on different rivers as well as on different mountains. Denham paints well the calm majestic Thames; Wilson, the rapid Spey; Scott, the immemorial and historic Forth; Burns, the wild lonely Lugar and the Doon; and Thomas Aird (see his exquisitely beautiful "River"), the pastoral Cluden. But the poet of the St. Lawrence, with Niagara flinging itself over its crag like a mad ocean—of the Ganges or the Orellana—has yet to be born, or at least has yet to bring forth his conceptions of such a stupendous object in poetry.

In "Cooper's Hill" we find well, if not fully exhibited, what were Denham's leading qualities—not high imagination or a fertile fancy, although in neither of these was he conspicuously deficient, but manly strength of thought and clearness of language. There are in him no quaintnesses, no crotchets, no conceits, and no involutions or affectations—all is transparent, masculine, and energetic. It is in these respects that he became a model to Dryden and Pope, and may even still be read with advantage for at least his style, which is

"Strong without rage, without o'erflowing full."

His translations we have included, not for their surpassing merit, but because, in the first place, there is little of our author extant, and we are happy to reprint every scrap of him we can find, and because again he, according to Dr. Johnson, was "one of the first that understood the necessity of emancipating translation from the drudgery of counting lines and interpreting single words." There has, indeed, been recently a reaction, attended in some cases with brilliant success—as in Bulwer's "Ballads of Schiller"—in favour of the literal and lineal method; but since such popular pieces as Dryden's "Virgil" and Pope's "Homer" have been written on Denham's plan, it is interesting to preserve the model, however rude, which they avowedly had in their eye.

His smaller pieces are not remarkable, unless we except his vigorous lines "On the Earl of Stafford's Trial and Death," containing such noble sentiments as these—

"Such was his force of eloquence, to make
The hearers more concern'd than he that spake,
Each seem'd to act that part he came to see,
And none was more a looker-on than he;
So did he move our passions, some were known
To wish for the defence, the crime their own.
Now private pity strove with public hate,
Reason with rage, and eloquence with fate."

Nor let us forget his verses on "Cowley's Death," which, although unequal, and in their praise exaggerated, yet are in parts exceedingly felicitous, as for instance, in the lines to which Macaulay, in his "Milton," refers:—

"To him no author was unknown,
Yet what he wrote was all his own;
He melted not the ancient gold,
Nor with Ben Jonson did make bold

To plunder all the Roman stores
Of poets and of orators;
Horace's wit and Virgil's state
He did not steal, but emulate!
And when he would like them appear,
Their garb, but not their clothes, did wear."

Such is true criticism, which, in our judgment, means clear, sharp, discriminating judgment expressed in the language and with the feelings of poetry.